A Harbour for the King

A Harbour for the King

The Loyalist Dream on the Island of Grand Manan

Wendy Dathan

Foreword by Eric Allaby

Chapel Street Editions

Publisher's Appreciation of Place

Chapel Street Editions exists within the unceded and unsurrendered territories of the Wolastoqiyik, Mi'kmaq, and Peskotomuhkati People. The work we do is born from the stories carried by this land and its inhabitants. The animals, plants, soil, water, and air make this place home for the Indigenous people, who belong to this land, for the descendants of those who took this land and made it a belonging, and for those who have since come from away. Chapel Street Editions holds a deep appreciation for our place within this land and the stories it tells. We honour the land's Indigenous caretakers and are grateful for their wisdom and guidance.

Published by
Chapel Street Editions
150 Chapel Street
Woodstock, NB E7M 1H4
chapelstreeteditions@gmail.com
www.chapelstreeteditions.com

ISBN: 978-1-988299-44-0

Library and Archives Canada Cataloguing in Publication

Title: A harbour for the king : the loyalist dream on the Island of Grand Manan / Wendy Dathan ; foreword by Eric Allaby.
Names: Dathan, Patricia Wendy, 1934- author.
Description: Includes bibliographical references.
Identifiers: Canadiana 20220389381 | ISBN 9781988299440 (softcover)
Subjects: LCSH: Grand Manan Island (N.B.)—History.
Classification: LCC FC2495.G73 D38 2022 | DDC 971.5/33—dc23

Cover photograph of Grand Harbour by Peter Cunningham

Book design by Brendan Helmuth

Chapel Street Editions, Ltd. gratefully acknowledges the financial support of the Department of Tourism, Heritage, and Culture, Province of New Brunswick

Dedication

To my friends and family for their loving support

and to Grand Manan for the joy
it has given me over all these years.

Table of Contents

Foreword

From the second floor of her Grand Manan home, Wendy Dathan has a commanding view of the Harbour that hosts her book. Depending on the time of tide, she might look out over shimmering water or placid mud flats with occasional defining ledge protrusions.

Looking from her window, the author can visualize back 250 years and picture the same shimmering water rising over uncharted mud flats. The peaceful power of the tide in the Harbour has inspired her to learn more about how it led to early settlement and fostered a self-supporting community.

In the early years of Island settlement, information was passed down through family stories and in letters saved and passed along. Newspapers were rare and in cities far away from this remote island in the Bay of Fundy, which was many sailing hours from the mainland.

Wendy brings to this book the skill and discipline needed to conduct effective research. She has knitted the sparse and separate yarns into an entertaining blanket of Harbour heritage that warms and inspires so many generations later. She breathes life and colour into long-empty names.

And it's not just the land transactions and material decisions that shape the growth of the community. We see characters of all kinds, many who are cooperative and community-minded and some less desirable individuals whose greed and nasty behaviour sets the community back in its efforts to progress together.

To use a crude analogy, Wendy has given us the ketchup, mustard, and relish that complete the bare burger of early historical fact and make for highly entertaining reading.

But it's not just the early years that she has enriched. More recent stories—stories carried in memory and passed along with remarkable fullness and detail—are preserved in this book. And if it were not for being preserved here, these stories would be lost with the passing of those who carried these rich memories.

Wendy is very thorough with her beloved village, house lot by house lot, recording shifts and trends, services and commercial activities that waxed and waned, the devastation of massive storms, and the resiliency in the building back, but not the same as before.

She traces family lines, recording offspring, siblings, and cousins that the residents of today's Grand Harbour can point to with affection and common identity.

As the author looks from her window, she doesn't project into the future as her book ends. She leaves the future in the capable hands of her friends and neighbours, confident that she has given them a sense of pride and heritage on which to continue building an even stronger way of life on Grand Manan.

Eric Allaby

Eric Allaby is the author of *Grand Manan* (1995) and *The Sea Wins: Shipwrecks of the Bay of Fundy* (November 2022)

Preface

The history of the settlement of the United Empire Loyalists on Grand Manan Island has been carefully covered in the excellent series of publications produced by the Grand Manan Historical Society. But in order to see and understand the full story it has always been necessary to search through the widely separate issues to obtain all the facts.

For this reason, this study delves into the background of the original Loyalists in coastal Maine and follows the timeline of their settlement and subsequent Island achievements in a single volume. Because Grand Harbour is located in the centre of the Island, and from which settlement expanded like ripples around a pond, it is a logical place in which to form a primary circle of interest. With this in mind, I decided to focus this book on the Harbour where the pioneer experiment began and follow the growth of the village around it. Perhaps this is not as arbitrary as it sounds; although in time the Island settlement spread to all corners of its habitable shores, it was not always due to the influence of the Loyalists as was so patently clear in Grand Harbour.

In coming here to settle, the Loyalists faced different problems than those in mainland New Brunswick. They were few in number and lacked the larger support of group influence and land mass. It is not for nothing that isolated Grand Manan was once described as "an island with Canada and America off its shores". But perhaps, like the islands of Montreal and Manhattan with their far greater population numbers, that very fact has given Grand Manan the strength of its "island-ness" in developing its own strong family-based character and unique approach to life and work.

The fortunes of Grand Manan may go up and down with ocean storms and the uncertain price of lobster, but its future depends, as it always has, on its ability to withstand and recover from the worst of times, its adaptability to change with new ideas and needs, and its history of building creatively on its foundation of faith and hard work.

Wendy Dathan,
Grand Manan, New Brunswick

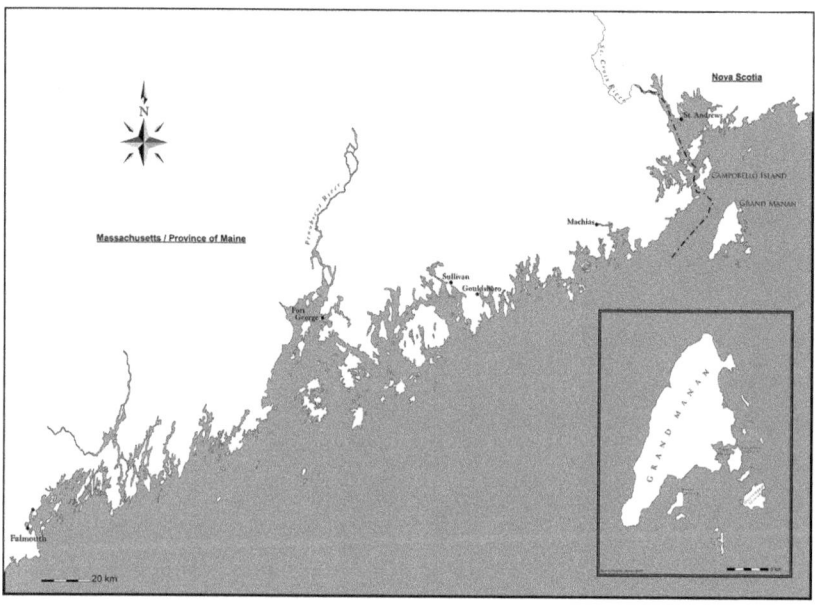

Fig. 1 – The Maine Coast and Grand Manan, 1779

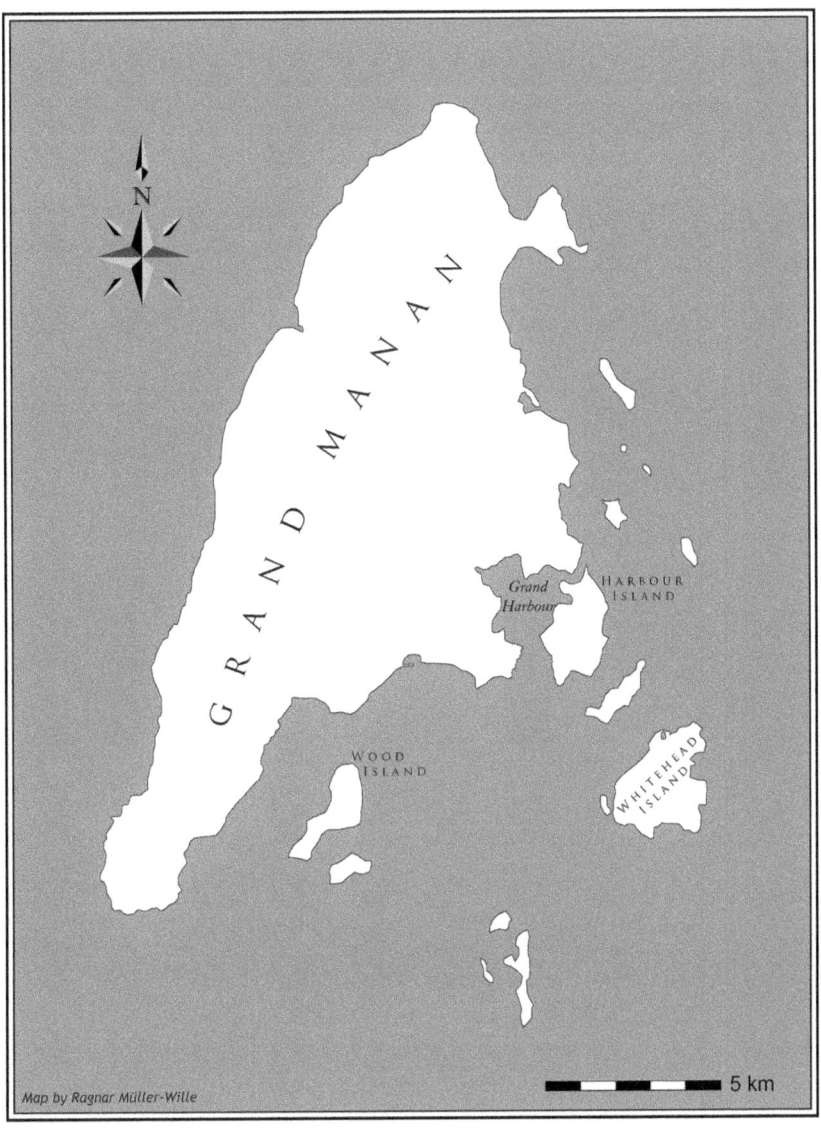

Fig. 2 – Grand Manan

Chapter I
In the Beginning

Grand Manan is a tiny triangle of land at the mouth of the Bay of Fundy, lying far closer to the scalloped coast of Maine than to the country of Canada to which she belongs. Grand Harbour, where our story begins, is tucked into her southeast corner, hidden by her petticoats of archipelago islets.

Grand Harbour is a harbour like no other. It is best described as a giant keyhole of a closed-in bay, cupped by the hollow of the main Island to the north and west, held fast to the south by the thumb of Ingalls Head, and shut firmly off from the sea to the east by tree-covered Ross Island that was known as Harbour Island when the first permanent settlers arrived. There is a minor seawater passage into and out of the Harbour on the north side of Ross Island, but the main entrance lies in the deepwater gap at Ingalls Head.

Although it was busy in the days of sail, there is little traffic in Grand Harbour now. It was J. G. Lorimer in his 1876 *History of the Islands and Islets in the Bay of Fundy* who first attacked the legitimacy of the Harbour name. Although he conceded that the sea view was delightful, he said "Grand Harbour only requires more depth, sufficient depth of water, at all times of tide, to make it deserving of the name 'Grand' in its widest use. It [It's shallowness] is an irredeemable obstacle at all times of tide."[1] The Harbour is not only shallow at most times of tide but is almost non-existent at lowest tide when a third or more of the basin is covered in oozing

---

1   Lorimer, J. G., 1876. *History of the Islands and Islets in the Bay of Fundy.* St. Stephen, NB; *St. Croix Courier.*

mudflats. So we must wait for high tide for Grand Harbour to really live up to its name.

The funnel-shaped Bay of Fundy is noted for its giant tides, with the North Atlantic sweeping in and up its sides in ever-increasing heights until reaching a climax of 53' at Burntcoat Head in the Minas Basin. Because of Grand Manan's position at the mouth of the Bay, we do not get the same tidal build-up as Burntcoat Head, but close to 28' can be impressive all the same and the volume of high-tide water that pours into Grand Harbour through the hole at Ingalls Head can be quite spectacular. In no time at all, the mudflats are gone. Gone are the low, uncertain edges of neap tide beaches and the seaweed-covered rocks where the gulls rest from their endless circling; gone are the freshwater pools formed by outpouring Bonney, Grand, and Bradbury Brooks as the saltwater fingers push higher and higher up their inner banks. It is truly at this beautiful time of tide that Grand Harbour lives up to its name.

In the old days of recent memory, this high tide sea level was the signal for action. Harbour fishing boats that had lain on their sides by the old wooden wharves—all that was left of them after the Groundhog Gale of 1976—were now happily afloat and ready to be stowed and set to travel to Ingalls Head and worlds beyond. At Murray Guptill's wharf on the north side of Grand Harbour, we could watch him and his sons as they prepared their dragger to depart for the scallop beds near Digby, Nova Scotia. The newly built or repaired vessels that were ready to go at Otis Green's Grand Manan Boats would now be launched, and there might be a delivery of sorts to the old wharf at Normie Green's MG Fisheries. But alas, that was yesterday. Today, just about everything that happens is around the corner in the ever-increasing wharf space at Ingalls Head.

So the Harbour has become a place for from-away birdwatchers. These visitors are not here in winter when the black ducks arrive to spend the coldest months among the ice cakes piling up near the shore and when the evening sunsets coat the Harbour in reflective red sky paint, nor are they here in early spring when the brant geese form feeding lines to feast on the eelgrass beds hidden below the wave surface. In late spring and early summer the birders are too focussed on the identity of the returning warblers to notice the cormorants drying their open wings on the posts near Gleason Green's old wharf on the road to Ingalls Head; it is only in late summer and fall when they bring their huge viewing scopes to watch the migrating shorebirds feeding busily along the edges of the flats. This is Nature's Grand Harbour, and it turns the mind backwards to a time when there was nothing here but sea mammals, birds and fish.

* * *

We do know there were people here earlier than we had expected. We are indebted to Spencer Fullerton Baird of the Smithsonian Institution in Washington, DC for giving us evidence of the first people to come and live in Grand Harbour, however briefly that might have been. Baird and his daughter Lucy came to the Harbour in the summer of 1869, miraculously just months before the disastrous Saxby Gale swept all signs of earlier activity into the sea. They came to dig up the seashell heaps that were left here 1000 to 2500 years ago by early inhabitants, possibly traders, from the Paleo-Indian period in Maine. From the seashell heap remains, Baird could see that these people had hunted seals, beaver and birds as well as eaten small fish and clams. There were many stone artefacts, including arrowheads and flint flakes. He found the most productive areas of search were at Newton's Point and Ingalls Head, but none of these middens were large, suggesting that there were not many people and they did not stay very long—but there is no doubt they were here.

We cannot know for certain when the descendant visitors, the Peskotomuhkati (Passamaquoddy) people of Maine, first came to the Harbour, but they certainly knew the Island well by the time

3

of Samuel de Champlain's arrival in the area in 1606 for they had named it "Munahnuk" from which he took the French equivalent of its present name. It is not until 1770 that we have definite proof about the presence of Peskotomuhkati summer residents in Grand Harbour but we can be sure that they were here for a long time before that. We are also sure that they would have come only in summer for there were no forest animals for them to hunt during the long months of winter.

In 1600, the coast of Maine had been long inhabited by Indigenous people—the Wolastoqey (Maliseet) to the north, the Peskotomuhkati lower down, and the Penobscot to the south. The Penobscots were generally a more settled people as they were better able to grow corn in milder latitudes, but those further north migrated seasonally, following the inland hunt in winter and the fishing coast in summer. Traditionally, they lived in small family groups during the hunting season and gathered into extended family bands and villages along the coast in summer where their round wigwams were ringed by canoes along the shore.

They were not the only people to occupy the coast of Maine during this period of time; the land claimers had arrived from Britain. In order to understand our Island heritage it is time to sail our minds away to that ragged curve of coastal inlets, bays, headlands, and islands of which we are almost but not quite a part. The first permanent English settlement in Maine was established in the early 1600s. The population grew slowly at first but by the time of the first official census in the 1760s, it had grown to 25,000 colonists. The "People of the Dawn", who had spent their lives in the post-glacial hunting forests, could only watch in dismay as the lumbermen cut down trees as if the supply was endless—the white pine soon gone for the ships' masts, the oaks and cedars for houses and industry. The softwoods were floated downstream to the sawmills, of which every community had at least one for a start. Dams were built on streams and rivers to produce the waterpower to run sawmills and gristmills, preventing the salmon— on which the Indigenous people depended—from reaching their upstream spawning and reproduction areas.

Yet the lumbermen did less damage than the farmers who bared the land to plant crops and graze their horses and cattle while the forest animals suffered and retreated. Trees were cut down for open fireplaces that consumed 30 to 40 cords of wood a year. They were cut to build fences, or burned to make additional ash to fertilize the fields, or simply because they were there in the way. It is recorded that where the forests had been cleared in Maine and the Maritimes, the land became "sunnier, windier, hotter, colder and drier." Streams and ponds dried up for parts of the year. The water table dropped and the soil became drier and poorer. Crops and vegetation suffered from drought.

Interestingly, the northern town of Machias, Maine, some 30 miles across the water from Grand Manan, began with the scarcity of hay in the drought of 1762. A party, from as far away as Scarborough in southern Maine, had visited the area in search of suitable grass and found a great quantity of it growing in the nearby saltmarsh. Others returned the following year and the new settlement began.

Among the newcomers who arrived in Machias in 1763 was a recently retired British Army officer reputed to have been the Ensign who had taken down the French colours at the fall of Detroit earlier that year. We must pay attention to this man for he will soon become important in the history of Grand Harbour and Grand Manan. Born in 1740 of Welsh descent in Pembroke, Connecticut (now Pembroke, Massachusetts), Joel Bonney would be described by his grandson as being "a very stout, able man, 6'1"tall, and remarkably fine looking". Following his retirement from the army, he had been engaged in the lumber business in Digdeguash near the present site of St. Andrews, New Brunswick but had found it impossible to procure food for his family. In Machias, he quickly became known as a capable carpenter and millright, with seven sawmills to his credit as the town grew up around him.

It must have been another drought year along the Maine coast in the summer of 1770, for that is when we have our first recorded sightings of people actually working in Grand Harbour. Capt. William Owen of Campobello Island rounded the corner of Ingalls Head and recorded in his journal that on 10 August 1770 he found a sloop at anchor inside the Harbour and a group of men who were busy cutting and making hay.

The Campobello party had begun the day by getting grounded at low tide outside Ingalls Head in the passage between Ross and Cheney Islands. The following account was recorded:

> *Here we met with John Wood Denny, an Indian and his Squaw, who to prevent our waiting the tide's ebbing, landed us in his Canoe on the north shore* [Indian Camp Point on Ross Island], *where we made a fire, boiled the teakettle, breakfasted, and shot some birds. At 9, the longboat being afloat and sufficient water in the passage, and the wind being at SW, it was with great difficulty we got through our sails and oars ... At 10 we landed on the point of the marsh on the south shore where we pitched the tent, made a fire and boiled the pot; we caught some young gulls, sheldrakes and dippers; and found here Captain Nichols, with a party of Mr. Lane's men from Gouldsboro cutting and making hay. We embarked at noon and ran up South-East, or (as it is commonly called) Grand Harbour; we called alongside the Haysloop from Gouldsboro, where the poor fellow that guarded her gave us some fine lobsters; then proceeded up to the head of the Harbour, where finding the tide had ebbed, we only filled a keg of fresh water at a small rivulet and turned down again. This Harbour is pretty spacious, and vessels may ride in security, with two fathoms at low water; but I would not recommend it to Vessels of burthen, unless in stress of weather, or real business.* [2]

---

2   The complete journal account can be followed in *The Grand Manan Historian*, No. VI, "Captain Owen's Visit in 1700." W. F. Ganong.

This extraordinarily specific information suddenly shines a light on the Harbour that had seemed to be hidden from sight for so long. It tells us that the residents of Maine—white fishermen-traders and Peskotomuhkati summer visitors—must have known it for many years before this important first recorded date.

*   *   *

By 1775, there was more than drought to worry about along the coast of Maine. The war that was to be known as the Revolutionary War or the American War of Independence had been staging bloody conflicts in Lexington and Concord, Massachusetts and the news was making itself felt as it filtered northwards. Machias was already a hotbed of revolutionary sentiment when a Loyalist merchant and his transport arrived from Boston on 2 June 1775 with the intention of trading goods and picking up a cargo of lumber for the British Army. The armed schooner HMS *Margaretta*, commanded by Lt. James Moore, escorted the merchant ship. Trading did not go well and the merchant was arrested. After the failure to seize Lt. Moore when he came ashore, the townspeople prepared to do battle. In the ensuing firefight, Moore was fatally wounded and his crew surrendered the *Margaretta*, which became the first British warship to be seized by the American side of the war.

With the success of their capture, Machias became the centre of anti-British activity in the Northeast. American privateers went out to harass the ports and shipping of Nova Scotia. An expedition led by Col. Jonathon Eddy attacked Fort Cumberland but was driven off by British troops. Early in 1777, Col. John Allan, a Nova Scotian who had been banished from Canada for his anti-British activity, was authorized by the Second Continental Congress to organize an expedition to establish a patriot presence in the area around the mouth of the St. John River. He left Machias with forty men and headed north where he managed to persuade a large number of Wolastoqiyiks to join the American cause and travel by canoe down to Machias through the inland waterway system of rivers and lakes.

Up to the time of the capture of the *Margaretta*, there had been little warlike activity along the coast in the south of Maine except for a skirmish in Falmouth, Massacheusetts (now Portland, Maine) in March 1775. This is a town of special interest to us because it was the home of Capt. and Mrs. Thomas Ross, soon to become permanent family settlers on Grand Manan. Born in the Glasgow area of Scotland, Capt. Ross had served as a British officer in the 78th Regiment of Foot before settling in Falmouth where he married Barbara Robinson on 9 December 1763. He became a master mariner and was taxed for owning one schooner (55 tons, L.O. 13.9) in 1766 when their first child was born. Over the years, the Rosses had five children—Barbara, Thomas, Elizabeth Tyng, John, and William—all living at home on Jones Lane while their father travelled frequently to and from the West Indies. At one point, Capt. Ross was part owner with George Lyde and Thomas Oxnard of the vessel *St. Vincent*, which may have been the Caribbean island where he acquired sugar interests.

Capt. Ross may or may not have been at home when the troubles began in his hometown. Loyalist builder, Capt. Samuel Coulson, had received a boycotted shipload of sail, rope and rigging from England and requested help to offload the cargo and repair the ship. HMS *Canceaux*, under the command of Lt. Henry Mowat, was dispatched from British-held Boston to ensure the success of this operation. Meanwhile, the local militia laid plans to capture the warship. On 2 March 1775, 50 militiamen led by Samuel Thomson, each wearing a sprig of spruce in their hats for identification, arrived secretly in small boats and captured Lt. Mowat when he went ashore to arrange for church service for his men. The crew on the *Canceaux* sent up warning gunpowder charges and threatened to shell the town unless Mowat was released. As many as 600 militiamen from the surrounding countryside gathered around as the townspeople anxiously negotiated to prevent a battle. Eventually, Mowat was returned to his ship and forced to leave port. But the militiamen, frustrated at not being able to secure the *Canceaux* for their use, looted the homes of Coulson and Loyalist Sheriff Tyng before going back to their home communities. We do not know if the Ross home was in any way targeted for vandalism but we do know there may have been some connection with the Sheriff because of the christening of one of their children as Elizabeth Tyng.

Back in Boston six months later, and four months after the news of the *Margaretta* capture in Machias, Mowat was ordered by Vice-Admiral Samuel Graves to "lay waste burn and destroy such Sea Port towns as are accessible to His Majesty's ships…in particular Machias where *Margaretta* was taken". In remembrance of his humiliating retreat from Falmouth only a short while earlier, Mowat was only too happy to make that his first port of call. HMS *Canceaux* left Boston in company with HMS *Halifax*, HMS *Cat*, bomb sloop HMS *Spitfire*, and supply ship HMS *Symmetry*; they anchored off Falmouth Harbour on 16 October 1775. The next day, Mowat moved into the inner harbour and sent one of his lieutenants ashore with a proclamation stating he was there to "execute a just punishment" for the town's state of rebellion. He gave them two hours to evacuate. The horrified townspeople sent a deputation to plead for mercy and Mowat promised to hold fire but only if the town swore an oath of allegiance to King George and surrendered all their small arms and gun carriages.

In response, the people of Falmouth began to move out of town. By 9 A.M. on the morning of 18 October 1775, the town appeared deserted and Mowat ordered the fleet to begin firing. For nine solid hours, incendiary cannonballs set fire to most of the deserted downtown houses and buildings. At the end of the day, he sent a landing party to set fire to any buildings that had survived. In all, more than 400 buildings and houses were recorded as damaged or destroyed and 15 small vessels were also destroyed or captured before Mowat's fleet departed, leaving the people of Falmouth to fend for themselves for the winter. Out of a population of 2500, more than 1000 were left homeless, including at least 160 families.

In the map of the town following the destruction we can see that the Ross family home had miraculously survived outside the area of fire. In all likelihood, Capt. Ross was away at the time, which would have saved his vessel, but we can only imagine the difficulties that he and his family went through in that winter of 1777–1778. By the following year, he was proscribed as a United Empire Loyalist sympathiser and forced to leave his family behind when he was banished to Halifax.

*   *   *

We move back to Machias now for the strange battle that was to avenge the seizure of HMS *Margaretta* and punish the town for its anti-British activities. Capt. Sir George Collier, 2nd in command at Halifax, sailed for Machias in late June 1777 in the frigate HMS *Rainbow*, accompanied by the brig HMS *Blonde* and joined en route by frigate HMS *Mermaid*, and sloop HMS *Hope*. Warned of the British arrival, and heartened by the addition of Col. Allan's Wolastoqiyik supporters, Col. Eddy had his militiamen lay a log boom across the Machias River and construct armed earthworks further inland. Collier arrived at the mouth of the river on 13 August 1777 and ordered the *Hope* and the *Blonde* to move upriver. The militia firefight prevented the British from attempting to land until the next morning when they went ashore under cover of fog, cut the log boom, captured a sloop carrying lumber, set fire to a storehouse, and seized supplies before returning to the ships.

There are conflicting stories about what happened next. Harassed by musket and cannon fire from the shore, the two ships moved up closer to the town while the militiamen and natives positioned themselves to protect potential landing sites. When darkness fell, Col. Allan's Wolastoqiyik supporters under Chief Joseph Neeala began an eerie chanting sound that echoed in the night and magnified the impression of their numbers. The warship crews, no doubt fearing they were hopelessly outnumbered, chose discretion over gunfire and quietly drifted back downriver with the tide. The *Blonde* briefly ran aground but was soon lifted by the rising waters. By morning, the British had gone. Both sides claimed victory when it was over but it was a hollow one for the British and Machias was never again threatened with attack for the rest of the war.

We must assume that Loyalist Joel Bonney took little or no active part in this Battle of Machias. He had steadfastly refused to bear arms or to take part in the American cause. By the winter of 1778–79 he felt so much "disturbed and harassed" that the time had come for he and his wife, together with his two brothers-in-law Abiel and James Sprague and their families, to find a safer place to live. In hopes of returning to life under the protection of the Crown, and armed with the belief that Grand Manan was uninhabited, except by the Peskotomuhkati, the Bonney-Sprague family set off for the Island in the early spring of 1779.

They rounded Ingalls Head and sailed into Grand Harbour, heading west near the shore until reaching a suitable corner on the southwest side that was bordered by what would later be named Bonney Brook. The site was a good choice and must have been close to the area where the men from Gouldsboro had been seen cutting hay so long ago. The newcomers had brought their milk cow as well as the inevitable barnyard hens. It was a good place for digging clams and fishing lobsters. It would not take long for a man of Joel Bonney's carpentry skills to build their first cabins on the shore.

Their activities had not gone unnoticed. It was not long before they received a serious warning dated 4 June 1779, addressed to Bonney from Col. Allan in Machias. A delegation of members of the Wolastoqey, Penobscot, and Peskotomuhkati tribes had made a complaint to the authorities that "a number of Inhabitants, Subjects of America, had Taken Possession and [were making] Improvements on an Island call'd Grand Manan, the property of said Indians." Upon examination it was found that Bonney and family had done as accused and "the most Evil Consequences might be Expected from such proceedings." The warning pointed out that the Island had occasioned much dispute between the courts of France and Great Britain, and even though Great Britain now claimed it as belonging to Acadia (Nova Scotia), it was guaranteed for the benefit of the Indians on behalf of the United States of America. The message from Col. Allan concluded as follows:

> *I do Warn you to leave without Delay the said Island as you will answer the Consiquence at your Peril, for a Breach of Treaty between the United States and said Tribes of Indians, and I have farther to warn you that the Greatiest Threats is thrown out against you by said Indians, the Execution of which will not be in the power of the Superintendent and Agent to prevent. Therefore if any difficulty befalls you or your Familys it will be your faults as you now have Sufficient Notice.*[3]

With such a dire warning hanging over their heads, it was imperative for the Bonneys and Spragues to confer with the Peskotomuhkatis, who agreed to let them remain and winter on the Island on condition of their paying ten dollars each. Somewhere over the years, the story of the price they paid became "ten dollars and one heifer". Whatever the real payment, they stayed only over the winter during which time Mrs. Bonney gave birth to a son, Alexander, who would always be known as the first white child born on Grand Manan. In the spring of 1780, the family moved back to Digdeguash where the town of Bonny River, New Brunswick, was later named after Joel Bonney.

*   *   *

The stage is now set for the last Maine sea battle to affect our small group of future first settlers, and this is the strangest of them all. Halfway between Machias and Falmouth lies Penobscot Bay, a large

---

3   The order for the Bonney family to leave the Island was reported by Jonas Howe in *The Grand Manan Historian*, No.V, "The History and Settlement of Grand Manan."

opening cut into the already deeply indented coastline that marks the estuary of the river which the British visualized as becoming the southern border of their new colony of New Ireland once the War of Independence was over. Jutting into this estuary is the point of land that the Penobscots had named, Majabigwaduce, shortened by the locals to Baggaduce. It is the site of today's town of Castine.

Early in July 1779, while the Bonney/Sprague families were trying to settle in Grand Harbour, a large British naval and military force under the command of General Francis McLean, Governor of Halifax and Commander of the 82nd Regiment of Foot, sailed into Baggaduce's wide harbour and landed 450 kilted soldiers from the 74th Regiment of Foot (the Argyleshire Highlanders), 200 lowlanders from the 82nd Regiment of Foot, and 50 gunners and engineers from the Royal Artillery and Engineers. Once offloaded of men and cargo, the HMS *Blonde* sailed for New York, leaving behind three transport ships and three sloops of war, the HMS *North*, HMS *Albany* and HMS *Nautilus*. The *Albany* was under the command of Capt. Henry Mowat, still somewhat in disgrace with his naval colleagues for his overly harsh treatment of the town of Falmouth.

The army took control of the village, consisting of about thirty houses, and began erecting a fort on one of the high points of the peninsula. Fort George, or Fort Baggaduce, was to be a roughly square earthen fort, 200' wide, with bulwarks projecting out 40' at the corners. For the most part, the walls would be 10' high, 20' on the eastward side, and it would include a palisade, a moat, and a gateway.

News of the British occupation of Maine was not well received in American controlled Boston. In short order, on 19 July 1779, an armada of 19 American warships and 24 transport vessels sailed north for Baggaduce carrying a multitude of American colonial marines and militiamen, with Massachusetts General Solomon Lovell in charge of the army, Continental Navy Capt. Dudley

Salonstall, seconded by General Peleg Wadsworth, in charge of naval action, and Col. Paul Revere in charge of artillery. Little did they know that the impressive Penobscot Expedition setting out so proudly that day was to be the worst naval disaster in American history until the fall of Pearl Harbour in World War II.

The British force at Baggaduce had barely begun to build the fort walls when the huge American expeditionary force sailed into the Harbour on 25 July 1779. The Brits clearly expected defeat when the Americans took control of a small battery on nearby Nautilus Island and managed to take over the steep headland a few hundred yards away from the fort. But then, to their amazement, the action stalled due to a leadership disagreement on the American side. With 600 men dug in on the headland, General Lovell would not attack the fort until Capt. Salonstall attacked the three British warships in the Harbour and Capt. Salonstall would not attack the British ships until General Lovell attacked the fort. While they argued and procrastinated for fatal days on end, the British soldiers continued to build up the walls of the fort and sent to New York for assistance.

On 13 August 1779, seven heavily armed British warships under the command of Sir George Collier sailed into Penobscot Bay. Anticipating a sea battle, General Lovell abandoned all his positions and retreated to his transports. What happened next is clearly above extraordinary. The next day, with all his ships and guns bearing broadside on the advancing British fleet, to everyone's astonishment Capt. Salonstall suddenly turned his ships about and fled up the river. Refusing to give them up to the British, he ordered the entire fleet of warships and transports to be sunk or scuttled or burned. The helpless crews and troops with most of their leaders were forced to climb the forest shores and walk back to Boston.

In all, the British lost 25 men while the Americans lost 43 ships and approximately 500 men. A committee of inquiry blamed the humiliating failure of the expedition on poor co-ordination between land and sea forces. A court martial was issued against Salonstall for his failure to engage the British naval forces and he was found to be primarily responsible, guilty of all charges, and dismissed from the Navy. Paul Revere, accused of disobedience and cowardice, was also court-martialled and dismissed from future naval service but eventually was cleared of all charges.

Once this sorry episode was over and the fort built to completion, the 82nd Regiment of Foot departed and General McLean returned to Halifax after guaranteeing to the villagers there would be no reprisals no matter which side they supported. From 1779 to 1783, Fort George became a magnet for United Empire Loyalists seeking safety under British rule. The officers of the fort had pleasant contact with the wealthier Loyalist arrivals among whom we recognize the name of Capt. Ross's partner in the ownership of the *St. Vincent*. Thomas Oxnard had fled Falmouth after the fire and had become a prominent businessman in the new "Capital of New Ireland". His name was listed as a client at Robert Pagan's general store that sold everything from food, tobacco and alcohol to clothing, household goods, and construction materials. His wife, who had been forced to stay behind, applied to visit her husband with their seven year old son in 1781, and the following year the Oxnard family was reunited when she received permission to move to Fort George with her family, two servant maids, and whatever goods the selectmen of Falmouth would allow.

Undoubtedly, the Oxnards would have befriended Moses Gerrish of Newbury, Massacheusetts, a graduate of Harvard College and one of the officers in the commissary department at Fort George. We have not been able to establish how or when Gerrish reached Fort George. It is doubtful that he received his commission in Halifax to arrive with the 78th or 82nd Regiments of Foot in time for the battle of the Penobscot Expedition. It is more likely he joined after travelling there at a later date.

It was B. F. da Costa, a visitor to Grand Manan in 1868, who learned from a report on the Loyalists in Maine that Moses Gerrish "possessed some ability". He also heard from someone who respected him that Gerrish had been a man who "would spread more sense on a sheet of paper" than any man of his acquaintance. Still, "he was not very persistent, and never amassed any property. He was *always going to do* something". We like him already, and we know that we will hear more of Moses Gerrish as he will soon be getting together with Thomas Oxnard and Capt. Thomas Ross to put in an application for settlement on the Island of Grand Manan.

* * *

Capt. Thomas Ross had been busy with his new life in Nova Scotia since his banishment from Falmouth in 1778. He had settled in Liverpool, further down the coast from Halifax, where his name appears in 1780 in John Leefe's story of *The Atlantic Privateers, 1749–1815*. Liverpool had at first been sympathetic to the American side of the war but turned against it after repeated attacks on local shipping interests and a direct attack on the town itself on 1 May 1778 when American privateers raided the town and destroyed and pillaged a number of houses and stores. From then on, Liverpool had enough of the Americans and turned to Halifax for protection, which came on 13 December 1778 in the form of a company of the King's Orange Rangers, along with several camp followers including women and children.

On 31 October 1779, Simeon Perkins, and others of the town's most prominent men in public life, launched their own privateer vessel, the *Lucy*, which had seen minor action before and was now in need of a new crew for her next voyage. On the morning of 11 May 1780, her captain went to Mrs. West's tavern for a "rendez-vous", a recruiting party for signing up a new crew. More recruits were still needed when he returned to the widow's popular establishment a week later, only to find that a rival rendez-vous was being held for Capt. Thomas Ross's privateer brig, *Resolution*.

To compete for attention, *Lucy's* captain gathered his recruits and paraded them through the streets of Liverpool. In the end, both vessels received an equal number of new hands throughout the day but the rivalry increased between the opposing crews as they grew larger. On 20 May 1779, the arguments got out of hand at the tavern where the men "hung around drinking and discussing the merits of their respective vessels". When it became a "Quarrel arising to a great height," according to Simeon Perkin's report, the King's Orange Rangers had to be called in to restore order.

It should be noted there was no sign of Capt. Thomas Ross at Mrs. West's tavern while all this was going on. He was represented by a man named Ben Collins who had been holding several rendez-vous events for the *Resolution* all the way down from Halifax where Capt. Ross was doubtless attending to the complicated and expensive process of becoming a Nova Scotia privateer. He would need an official letter of marque, for which there were strict rules, and the owners of the vessel would have to pay large sums of money in the form of a bond. Unlike the unlawful activity of unfettered piracy, the privateers could only operate in wartime and every captured ship had to be sailed to the Nova Scotia homeport and turned over to the court of Vice-Admiralty. There had to be proof that the captured vessel belonged to His Majesty's enemies or to people trading with them. Ship and cargo were then sold at public auction and the owners had to pay legal fees out of the prize money, from which the captain and crew might receive little more or sometimes even less than normal ship's pay. Such were the questionable rewards of being a privateer.

Turning back to the recruitment results of the opposing privateer ships in Liverpool, once the *Lucy* had signed up enough crew members from as far away as Argyle and Yarmouth, she cruised the Gulf of Maine for three weeks in June and July before sending home the disappointing prize of five empty schooners "of small value" and a brig loaded with salt.

For the *Resolution*, the results were more than disappointing; they were disastrous. On 13 July 1780, Simeon Perkins recorded in his diary that off Halifax, Captain Thomas Ross's *Resolution*

> *had a Severe engagement Near the Light House (Sambro) with the Ship 'Viper', Captain Williams, from Boston for 3 glasses. Capt. Ross lost 8 or 9 men, and his vessel much Disabled…Among the killed is Mr. Raphael Wheeler and Silas Harlow of this Town and John Caldwell of this Neighbourhood.* [4]

On receiving the news in Falmouth of her husband's disaster near Halifax, Barbara Ross changed her earlier 1779 request to be transferred to New York and petitioned the House of Representatives in Massachusetts on 1 September 1780 to go to Halifax where she had lately been informed that her husband was now residing. In her application, she stated that Captain Arthur McLellan was willing to take her there in the schooner *Hazard* and prayed that he might be commissioned with the necessary papers to carry her and her family, consisting of one maid and five children.

There was an additional request to go on the same vessel from a merchant in Casco Bay, one Richard Codman, who claimed that Capt. Thomas Ross, formerly of Falmouth but now of Halifax, owed him a large sum of money amounting to about twelve hundred pounds sterling, which Ross was willing to settle if Codman could obtain permission to go to Halifax for that purpose. All requests were approved on 8 September 1780 with the stipulation that Barbara Ross and her children were not to return to Massachusetts again without permission from the General Court.

We may never know whether or not the *Resolution* could be made seaworthy again or if Capt. Ross returned to the difficult life of

---

4   Coverage of Captain Ross and the *Resolution* in Simeon Perkin's diary can be followed in *The Atlantic Privateers: Their Story, 1749–1815* by John Leefe. Petheric Press, Halifax, NS, 1978.

a privateer for the duration of the war, but we can be sure he would never be without a vessel for very long. Reunited with his family, whom he would in time move down to Liverpool, he would doubtless soon be back at sea in some vessel in some capacity.

At one or more points in time, it is expected he would find time and reason to visit Fort George in order to confer with Moses Gerrish and Thomas Oxnard about the plans for Grand Manan settlement. By the time the War of Independence ended in September 1783, Moses Gerrish, Thomas Ross and Thomas Oxnard, as well as John Jones, Peter Jones, "and others" had signed the group's application for the licence of occupation of the Island. The licence was for "Fifty Families to Occupy during pleasure the Island of Grand Manan and the small islands Adjacent in the Fishery with Liberty of Cutting Flake Stuff and Timber for Building Hutts and Stores, and Wood for firing".[5] His Excellency John Parr, Captain General and Governor in Chief In and Over His Majesty's Province of Nova Scotia and its Dependencies granted the licence on 31 December 1783.

The Treaty of Paris agreement to end the war did not accede to the British claim to the land as far south as the Penobscot River, so the Loyalist haven at Fort George could no longer be a safe part of a British colony named New Ireland. The Fort was finally evacuated in January 1784. In October 1783, a flotilla of boats was organized to ferry the Loyalists who wished to leave the settlement to travel above the Canadian boundary of the St. Croix River. It is believed that the Oxnard family opted to stay in Fort George.

In *The Diverting History of a Loyalist Town*, Grace Helen Mowat paints a charmingly imagined portrait of the arrival of the Penobscot Loyalists in St. Andrews in 1783. After the ships had anchored and small boats lowered, she writes:

---

5   "Licence of Occupation, 1783." *The Grand Manan Historian* No. V.

> *The gallant gentlemen, in their powdered wigs and plum-coloured coats and three-cornered hats, helped the ladies to alight. How quaint and delightful a picture. Those courteous gentlemen and gentle and courageous ladies, in silks and quilted petticoats, tripping up over the sands to their new homes ... with all their household goods, priceless mahogany and silver plate, damask and linen, family portraits, and heavy trunks, brass-studded and covered with calf skin, their servants and coloured slaves.*[6]

Quaint and delightful indeed! These gentlefolk may well be happy living in St. Andrews, but we must look behind them for the kind of Loyalists we need on Grand Manan. We need men and women with the strength and courage to make a new home in the wilderness if we expect success in settling our isolated Island; preferably plain folk with manual skills like the Bonneys and Spragues.

Moses Gerrish would have sailed with the 74th Regiment of Fleet that was disbanded once reaching St. Andrews. During the winter, he would have time to organize the necessary details for the following year while possibly staying with an old friend from his hometown of Newbury, Massachusetts. William Cheney had been living on Indian Island until moving to a farm outside St. Andrews with his wife and eleven children. By 1784, he and his son William Jr. had been approved for a land grant on an island just outside Grand Harbour, soon to be known as Cheney Island; it would not be long before Gerrish and the Cheneys would be neighbours in a new environment.

---

6   Mowat, Grace Helen, 1953. *The Diverting History of a Loyalist Town.* Fredericton, NB; Brunswick Press.

Chapter II

Harbour Home

On the morning of 6 May 1784, Capt. Thomas Ross, Moses Gerrish, John Jones "and others" sailed past Ingalls Head into Grand Harbour and moored their large vessel in the deeper waters off Harbour Island. We can imagine the stillness of that scene across the uninhabited Harbour—the forest silence of the trees and the lap of quiet water—before the noise of disembarkation. Previously, this scene had only been briefly interrupted by the first settlement attempt and the occasional summer visits of the Peskotomuhkati people in their canoes.

According to the McDonald Report of 1804, the licensees brought two unnamed Loyalist families as well as several workers whom Gerrish may well have chosen for their skills as lumbermen, carpenters, fishermen or cooks. We have no details of the plans for the two additional families, but we can imagine the scene on arrival. The first order of business would be to clear out some of the forest trees and erect brush shelters for cooking, sleeping and storage arrangements until these could be replaced by the first winter cabins. The roughest of these cabins might be the traditional pioneer kind with outer walls of logs or sawn lumber built around an earthen floor, with space for a cooking fire in the middle and a hole in the ceiling for the smoke to go out, but it is likely that those built for Gerrish and Ross would be less primitive from the start.

We can imagine that Moses Gerrish would be left to supervise the work of building the necessary accommodation and clearing the land to plant root vegetables, beans, and corn as well as setting up the first fishery with small boats to go out on the Harbour. Capt. Ross made several trips to the mainland to bring back additional supplies. However that first year went, it must have gone well, because life on Harbour Island had advanced sufficiently by the summer of 1785 for Capt. Ross to sail to Liverpool to bring his family back to live with him.

The Ross family had done well in Liverpool. In 1783, Barbara, the oldest daughter, had been married at age sixteen to a newly arrived British surgeon, Dr. Stephen Thomas. The other children had grown and thrived in a stepladder of ages from oldest son Thomas down to youngest daughter Margaret, who must have been born in Nova Scotia. It would seem obvious from the moment of their arrival in Grand Harbour that there was nothing for Dr. Thomas to do at this early pioneer stage, in spite of the fact that he is often claimed as the Island's first doctor. It was not long before he and his wife set off for England in order for him to complete another two years of surgical training. They eventually returned to settle in Falmouth, Massachusetts, to live perhaps in the old Ross house on Jones Lane.

We can certainly imagine the transformation in the Capt. Ross home with Mrs. Ross soon at work with the help of her younger daughters and long-time maid. There was so much to be done to care for such a large household, with the constant need to cook and clean and do laundry, to make lye soap for cleaning and washing purposes, to make candles for eventide, to churn butter and make cheese, to tend a garden and gather wild blueberries, to put up preserves, to spin and weave and sew cloth to make clothes for herself and the children, and to quilt bright coverings for all their beds. As for the boys, who may well have been in charge of fetching water and keeping the fire going, young Thomas would be learning to be a mariner like his father while younger brother John was more interested in learning about dairy farming and youngest brother William was happiest messing about with boats and helping the men fishing.

In his excellent, illustrated book, *Grand Manan*, Eric Allaby tells us that the first fishing was mainly done by hook and line to catch mackerel, hake, cod, and pollock.[7] To catch herring for bait, the men went out at night in small boats equipped with flares dipped in oil and "torched" the waters to attract the fish to the surface where they were scooped up in dip nets. We do not know how soon it may have taken for the first settlers to try making stone weirs to catch the herring that came into the Harbour at high tide and were trapped inside when the tide receded, but the remains of one such weir has been found at Ingalls Head. Arthur Fleet remembered that there were more in Cheney Passage that were still in use when Ross Island was inhabited by eight families early in the twentieth century. The first smokehouses to cure the herring may well have evolved from the earliest cabins. A settler who came to the south of the Island in January 1805 found the land he had been given already had a log cabin and a "smoakhouse" on it.

Activities similar to those on Harbour Island were also taking place in the home and on the land of the Cheney family on their island southeast of Ingalls Head. Mrs. Cheney was expecting her twelfth

7   Allaby, Eric, 1984. *Grand Manan*. Grand Manan, NB; Grand Manan Museum.

Fig. 3 – Torching at night for small herring, mid-1800s.

child, Barbara, who would become the first white female born on Grand Manan. William Cheney was busy establishing a herd of cattle on his 200 acres of land, as well as using an additional 200 acres of grazing land on nearby unoccupied White Head Island, accessed by crossing what came to be known as Cow Passage at low tide. Friendly Peskotomuhkati families often visited the Cheney family in summer. They would cross over from their camp at the southern tip of Harbour Island and spend the night in one of the cabins.

Moses Gerrish was by now living quietly in his home on the lot next to the Thomas Ross family. The Gerrish house is depicted in a long ago sketch as being one-storey with a gable roof framed by a chimney on each end. The front door, facing the Harbour, had windows on each side so he could watch the view from the cove.

Moses Gerrish had been busy from the beginning with Island maps, drawing up allotments of land, measured in "chains", to fill out the requirements of supplying fifty families with lots to complete the licence of occupation. Although a headland southwest of Ingalls Head was named Ox Head in honour of Thomas Oxnard, neither he nor Peter Jones ever attempted to fulfill their part in the Island settlement. John Jones came in the beginning but within two years he had sold his share to James and Patrick McMaster, past merchants of Boston, and even they failed to take possession. It was not easy to establish a footing in this isolated location, but with the help of Capt. Ross, who sought to bring newcomers to the Island, Gerrish continued to do what he could to find suitable applicants to populate the land.

He was overseeing the occupation of the outlying islands as well as the Harbour, including the one farthest out, south of White Head, where John and Susannah Kent and their children put down roots. Like the Cheneys, they may well have been old friends of Gerrish. A great number of allotments were allocated to the children of the Ross family. William Ross received Wood Island, which he leased for sheep farming to newly arrived Loyalist William Green.

His brother, John, received High Duck and Harbour Islands. Additional land was also allocated to two of the older Ross daughters, with Barbara Thomas receiving a large lot in North Head near Whale Cove and Elizabeth (Betsy) Ross acquiring two in Grand Harbour, one on the north side bordered by Bradbury Brook and the other at Ingalls Head to the south.

Of all the Ross family members to receive lots, it was John Ross who really husbanded his land, clearing it to graze his dairy cattle and starting a business of making and selling butter. A large saltmarsh

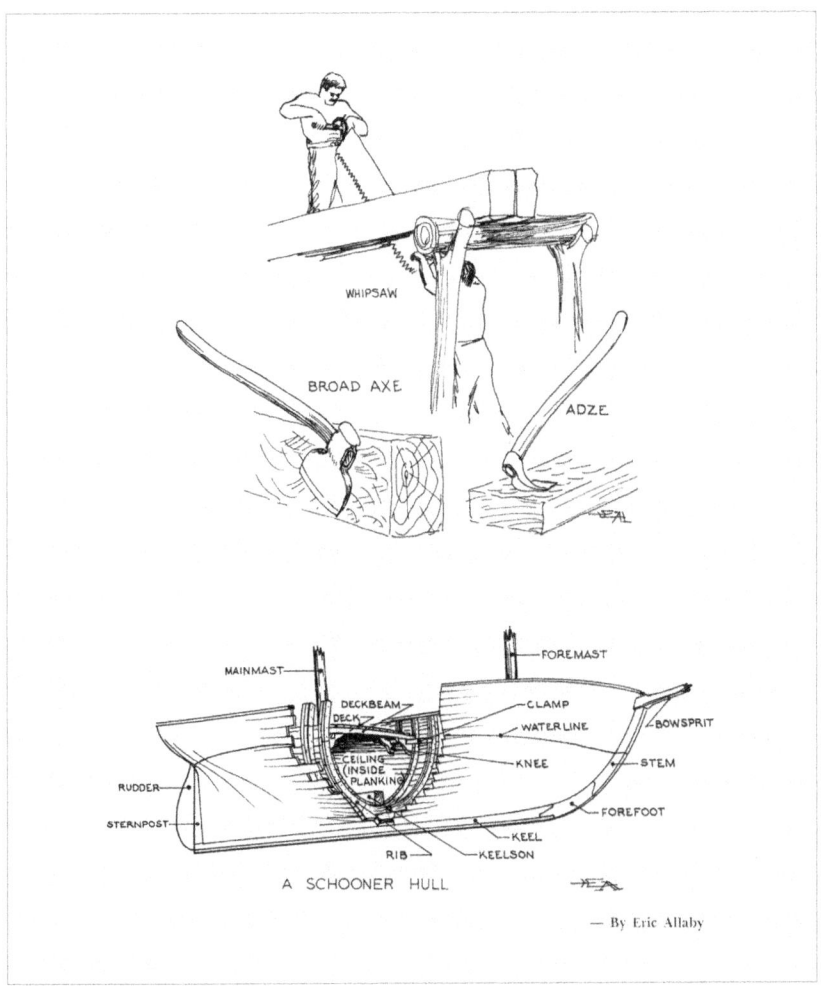

Fig. 4 – Shipbuilding tools and construction detail. Sketch by Eric Allaby.

in the area of the Thoroughfare adjacent to Ross Island would have been an important source of hay. It has since been drowned by the rising sea level.

Not all who received land had done much by way of improvements in the first years of settlement but that was certainly not the case with the Wooster and Ingalls families who arrived in Grand Harbour in 1799. Oliver Wooster's father had originated from Gerrish's hometown of Newburyport before taking his family to live in Sullivan, Maine after the war. Oliver had married Sarah Preble Newton in 1798. They came to Grand Manan the following year, closely followed by John Ingalls and his wife Rebecca Belcher Newton and family. They became co-owners of a large lot near Grand Brook in the centre of the village. It is believed that Sarah Preble Newton and Rebecca Belcher Newton were sisters and their father, Philip Newton, may have also come to Grand Manan at this time.

In his 1804 survey of Grand Manan, Donald McDonald reported that John Ingalls (6 in the family) and Oliver Wooster (4 in the family), now six years settled, were useful, industrious settlers on their lot #34 of 137 acres that covered roughly a third of the present village of Grand Harbour. They had purchased another small lot of 30 acres from former settlers and were involved with the Ross family in the operation of a saw mill on Grand Brook as well as being involved in the construction of a schooner of about 100 tons burden. In addition, Oliver Wooster had been granted Lot #40 with several acres of woodland that also showed improvement. Before long, he and his oldest son Oliver would be owning a shipyard, running a kiln to make bricks from the excellent Grand Brook clay, and operating a tannery for making boots. After a mere twenty years, Grand Harbour Village was making important strides toward success.

* * *

Eighteen hundred and four was a banner year for the advancement of Grand Manan Island as a whole. The first signs of other future villages and hamlets could be seen in the activities of the Flaggs in North Head, the Woodbury's saw mill in Castalia, the shipbuilding being undertaken by Joel Ingersoll in Woodwards Cove, and the burgeoning establishment of Seal Cove under the energetic leadership of Dr. John Faxon.

Back in the Harbour, eight lots had already been granted around the shore in 1804, beginning with Lot #30 at the east end of the Thoroughfare belonging to Simeon Littlejohn, a man of whom we know very little. There had been two brothers named John and Peter Littlejohn stationed at Fort George with Moses Gerrish who had travelled with him to St. Andrews as part of the Penobscot Association, but no one has been able to establish Simeon's relationship with them. He may have been one of the single labourers who accompanied Gerrish and Ross to the Island because his lot is very small, only 10 acres, and generally unfit for purposes of cultivation. We have only to drive along the road framing what is left of Lot #30 today to find it used mainly for commercial purposes and to realize that the low, stony shoreline and poorly drained peat bogs would have challenged the bravest of souls.

Moving west to Lot #31, we can see the difference immediately as we climb the hill to the rich meadowland and tall trees that once belonged to the Gubtail family. John Gubtail, later to be Guptill when the family name was changed, was one of three brothers who came to Grand Manan from Gouldsboro, Maine. According to the family records, they came in 1779, but since, at that time, they were all serving in branches of the American military forces in the Revolutionary War against the British, the date is obviously incorrect, as was their claim to be Penobscot Loyalists. However, they were young and strong and it mattered little to Moses Gerrish if they were willing to work the land.

John Gubtail would have Lot #31 to improve in his own good time, his brother, William, another lot in North Head, while brother, Abijah, would have a lot eventually even if he was criticized sharply by Donald McDonald in 1804 for occupying the one restricted for public use until he received his own land grant. These young men were the kind of settlers who would form the backbone of the Island economy, hardworking farmer-fishermen dividing their time between land and sea as the needs and seasons dictated. If we look into the future from the time of settlement we can find two outstanding descendants who will bring honour and fame to the family name.

Moving west around the Harbour to Lot #32, which belonged to Elizabeth Ross, we can see the land here is good but like her land on Ingalls Head we can say little about its use for the time being. Lot #33 begins on the other side of Bradbury Brook, around the turn heading towards the village. It is a large lot shared by Edmund Cheney, son of William Cheney, and John Doggett, another family name that will change in time to become Daggett.

The Daggetts were a proud family with a long history of settlement in North America, related on one side to the newcomers on the Mayflower and on the other to an ancestor who came on the Mary Jane and settled in Massachusetts in 1637. Over the years, their descendants held high official positions in many towns, as well as being credited with the founding of Fort Worth, Texas, and Liverpool, Nova Scotia. According to a newspaper clipping published at the end of a family celebration in August 1957, there still exists in Boston, on the corner of Hollis and Tremont, a portion of the old Daggett homestead of which one room is pointed out as the place where Bostonians disguised themselves as Indians to carry out the famous tea party in Boston Harbour.

The large Cheney/Doggett property continues westwards to adjoin Lot #34, the equally large one belonging to the Woosters and Ingalls. Together, these two properties form the centre of Grand

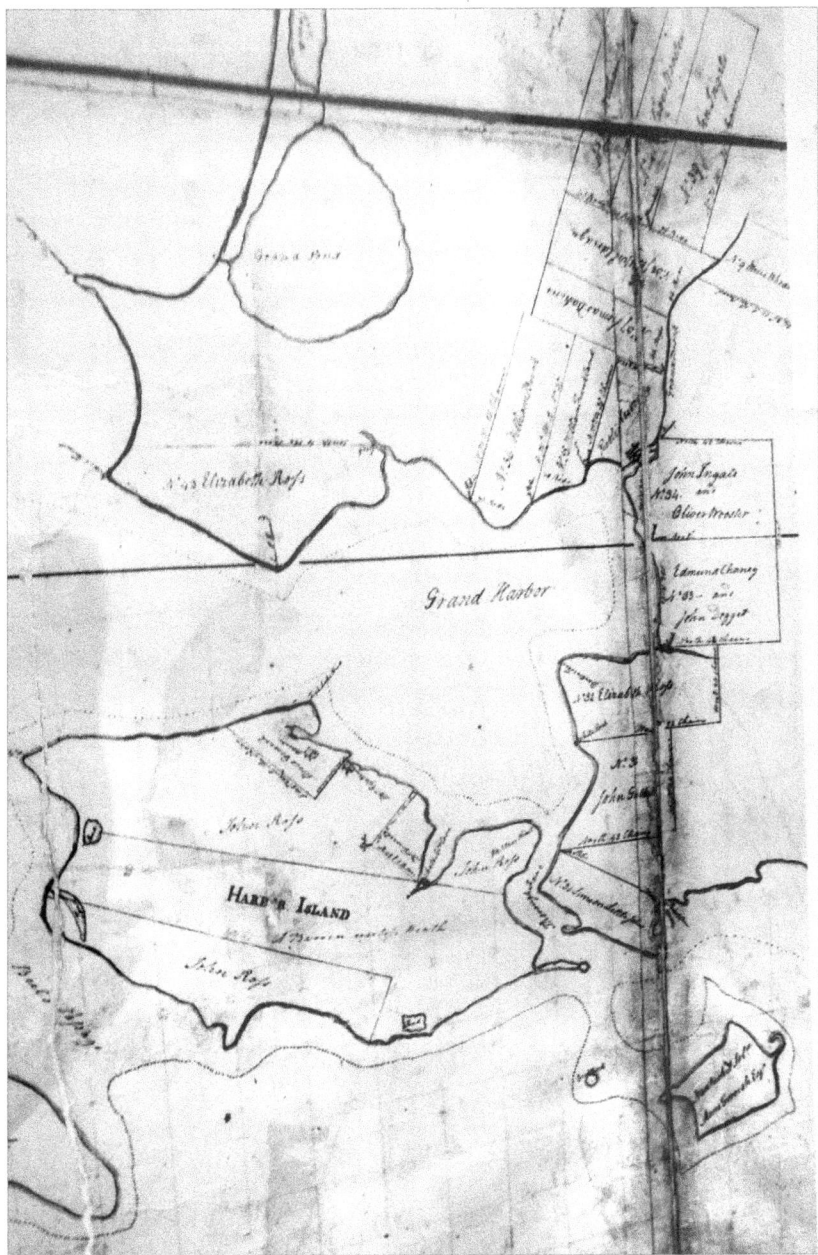

Fig. 5 – Map of land grants around Grand Harbour, early 1800s.

Harbour Village as we know it today; beyond that, lies Grand
Brook and the turn around the corner towards Ingalls Head. Here
we find the lot designated as public land, waiting for a church to

be erected. Further on is the 60-acre Lot #35 that was allocated to William and Ann Frankland and their family of six children on their arrival from St. Andrews in 1801.

William Frankland was born in Whitby, Yorkshire, that grey sea-girt town on the edge of the North Sea, which famous explorer James Cook also called home. On 27 October 1789, William Frankland married Ann Ross, the daughter of an Englishman named Capt. Thomas Ross who lived in St. Andrews. Due to the confusion of names, the genealogical files in the Grand Manan Archives are full of misleading speculation that Ann Ross was the daughter of Capt. Thomas Ross of Harbour Island, Grand Manan, but our Capt. Ross was a Scotsman from Glasgow who had no daughter named Ann.

According to the 1806 report by the Deputy Land Surveyor, Donald McDonald, William Frankland was an asset to the young community as "a seaman, a navigator, a ship carpenter, of undoubted loyalty, and well acquainted with the navigation of the Bay of Fundy", but his lot was of "so poor a quality that it in great measure impoverished him". In 1804, Frankland petitioned for the whole or part of White Head Island, by which time the family had increased to eight children. Hoping to pass his present lot to his two oldest boys if he succeeded, the family finally moved to White Head in 1805. Much of White Head was as poor quality as Lot #35 except for the marsh on the northern side where salt hay could be cut and the forty acres around Gull Cove where Frankland cleared a couple of acres and built a small log cabin near the shore.

Gull Cove would become a calling point for local cod fishermen returning from the nearby Grand Banks, and in time Frankland opened a store selling fishing supplies and built two ships in the cove, *Deana* and *Twin Sisters*. In later years, Frankland would be made famous by the arrival of naturalist John James Audubon and his merry band of young gentlemen when they visited Gull Cove on 22 May 1833 at the start of their adventurous trip to collect birds in

Labrador. In his celebrated *Birds of America,* Audubon mentions his visit with Frankland and his surprise at finding herring gulls nesting in trees on White Head, a habit they are believed to have adapted due to heavy human predation of their eggs during the nesting season and discontinued after moving to more remote islands.

Despite his removal to White Head Island, William Frankland remained a force for good in Grand Harbour. He was a magistrate for Charlotte County and served as warden when the Church of England was built on Lot #3 in 1824. He was Sub-Collector of Customs for Grand Manan and Justice of the Peace in 1832. He was Deputy Treasurer for collection of Light dues from ships entering the Bay of Fundy in 1835.

Alas, we have no such record of either good or bad for Frankland's Grand Harbour neighbour on Lot #36. Who William Burke was and what he did is shrouded in the annals of time. As we continue east to Ingalls Head, we have another mystery in the huge piece of land belonging to Elizabeth Ross. We do not know how that land was being used in the beginning. Perhaps parts of it were leased to the men who worked for the Ross family. It would be another 45 years before Turner Ingalls built the first permanent home on Ingalls Head.

*   *   *

By now, Capt. Ross and his son Thomas had resumed trade with the British West Indies. Whether they went as private traders, or as privateers during the many Caribbean wars, it was always a difficult and dangerous undertaking. They would face hurricanes on the one hand and the fierce tropical sun on the other. Sometimes drinking water or firewood for cooking stoves would run short. Harbours were few and hidden reefs made some dangerous. There was the constant threat of the deadly fever called "yellow Jack". Whole crews fell ill and many men died. In times of marine warfare, they faced the additional danger of being boarded by enemy ships and taken captive.

In the year 1800, the *Frances Mary* had sailed out of Liverpool and was captured on the Spanish Main. Capture by the French meant the ship would be taken to Guadeloupe or Martinique where the men would be thrown into foul stone dungeons as prisoners of war. If they tried to escape, they were tied to the walls. Only rarely did anyone manage to get away and return to their home in faraway Nova Scotia.

It did not take long for tragedy to strike the Ross family. We learn from a letter in the Ross family files in The Grand Manan Archives written 29 February 1903 by Fred Ware, grandson of Barbara and Stephen Thomas, that his great-grandfather died at sea from yellow fever in 1806. Earlier, Ware wrote,

> *...he and his boy had money in the West Indies. They sailed under the English flag. Thomas (Jr.) went out there to get their earnings they had for years—he got the money and got (to) sea and was taken prisoner by some nation that was at war with England so he lost all his money... He never came home, he died at sea.*

Danger on the high seas came home to the Island again in 1812 when a new war between England and America began. The Bay of Fundy was besieged by American privateers buzzing like hornets around Grand Manan until the British Navy brought in cruisers to deal with the situation. One privateer vessel managed to slip unseen into Grand Harbour and seize a vessel riding quietly at anchor in Bonney Brook. J. G. Lorimer tells us that the privateers,

> *having caught one vessel, felt eager for another, and... pounced upon [the] schooner Sally, owned by Wooster and Ingalls, who, anticipating a visit from the Yankee privateers, had removed a plank from [the] bottom, which of course rendered the craft altogether unseaworthy. The privateers attempted to repair damages, but failed in the attempt, and Wooster and Ingalls were left in possession.*[8]

---

8   Lorimer, J. G., 1876. *History of the Islands and Islets in the Bay of Fundy.* St. Stephen, NB; St. Croix Courier.

Fig. 6 – Sailing ships historically associated with Grand Manan fishing and trade. Sketch by Eric Allaby.

We do not know if Mrs. Ross left Grand Manan after her husband died, taking her younger daughters with her; their names do not appear on a later census. Our only clue as to their disappearance is in Fred Ware's letter when he says that his mother had two aunts, Aunt Campbell and Aunt Paddock, which can only be the married names of Elizabeth and Margaret Ross. He also had sad news to report about the demise of Dr. Stephen Thomas in Falmouth, Massachusetts, in 1815. "He had to go down to one of the ports in the night and it stormed and he took cold which caused his death." Barbara Thomas returned to Grand Manan with her children and settled on her land in North Head, although some of them chose to live with their Uncle John in Grand Harbour.

By now, John Ross had built a big house on his property on Harbour Island, a house that from all accounts was filled with priceless mahogany furniture and a great many books, all beautifully bound. He had never married and apparently had no such intention. His dairy business was flourishing and he was employing as many as fifteen women to make butter and cheese that he shipped to Saint John for sale. He was also expanding his fishing enterprises on High Duck Island.

William Ross and his wife, Clarissa, continued to live in the old Capt. Ross house on Harbour Island. Like his father and older brother before him, William Ross had become a master mariner but there is no mention of further adventures in the Caribbean. The pioneer days were over on the Island and William had been there for most of his rough and ready life. He was not popular with everyone when he assumed he could take on his father's leadership role. Moses Gerrish is reported as confiding in a letter to a friend in 1826, "those who have sense and property sufficient to live comfortably, never were Ross's friends and never will be." [9]

* * *

By 1820, there was a strong sense among the families of wealth and prominence in Grand Harbour that it was time to fulfill their United Empire Loyalist dreams of having a school and church in the thriving community. They already had a small school. Lot #3 had been held in reserve for a church. With their devotion to the Crown, the religion of choice would be the Church of England.

---

9   Ross family papers. Grand Manan Archive, Grand Manan Museum. Grand Manan, NB.

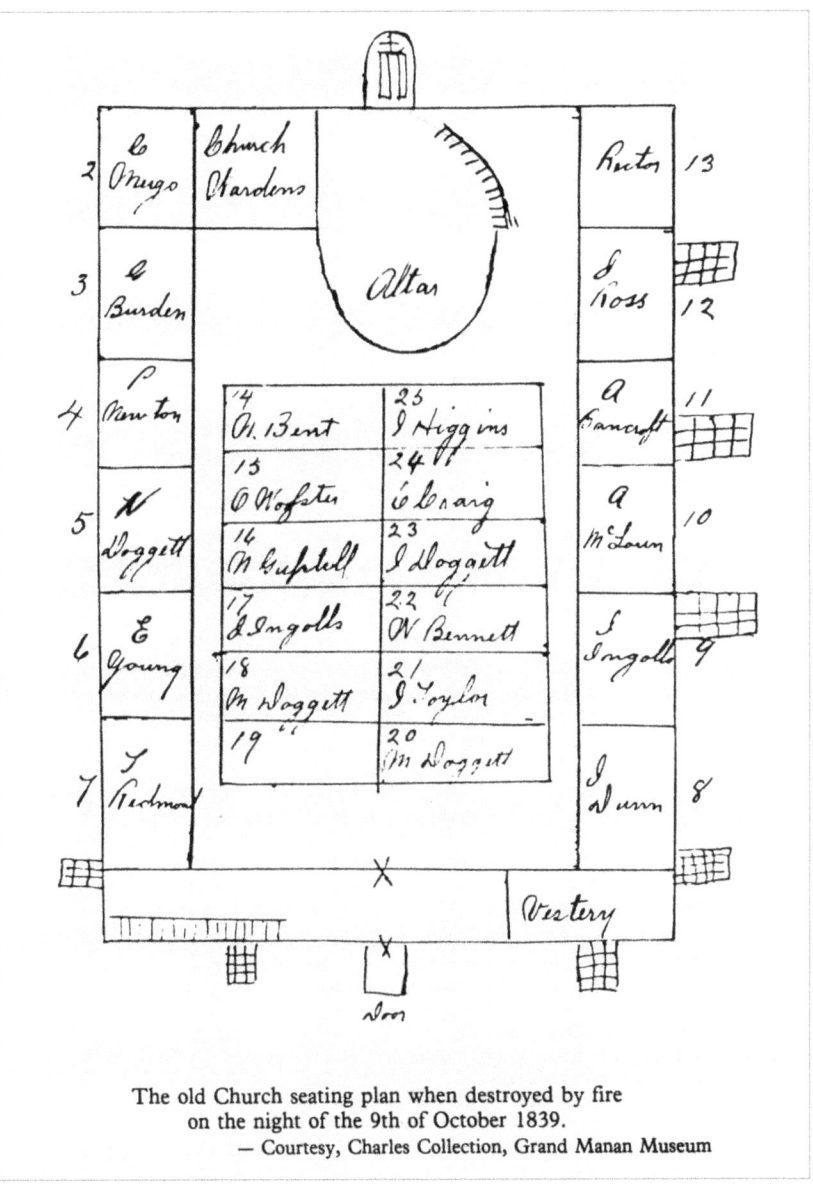

The old Church seating plan when destroyed by fire
on the night of the 9th of October 1839.
— Courtesy, Charles Collection, Grand Manan Museum

Fig. 7 – St. Paul's Anglican family pews in first church building, 1824.

We are indebted to the Rev. Wade L. Reppert for his careful research into the background and history of St. Paul's Anglican Church.[10] The effort to establish a church began with letters, applications, and pleas to the Society for the Propagation of the Gospel (SPG) even before the first recorded arrival of a clergyman travelling to Grand Manan to conduct services and baptize converts. Dr. Jerome Alley, the zealous rector at St. Andrews, arrived on the last Sunday in July 1820 to stay in the home of Capt. and Mrs. Thomas Ross and travel all over the Island to spread the word of the gospel. He returned on 18 September, once again to travel everywhere, even as far as White Head and Wood Islands, by which time he had baptized 85 children and 37 adults and raised the encouraging sum of £254 to build a new church in Grand Harbour.

It would take three years for St. Paul's to open for worship. Logs had to be cut and hauled to the site, with work having to stop entirely during an exceptionally severe winter. The end result of all their hard work was a plain, unpainted, clapboard building enclosing neat rows of pews, a gallery, an altar and a reading desk. We have only to read the names on the reserved pews, names like Doggett, Wooster, Guptill, Newton, Ross and Ingalls, to know that our most successful earliest settlers had indeed become supporters of this important religious endeavour. William Frankland became the first Church Warden. It teases the mind to wonder if he compared St. Paul's with his big old church in long ago Whitby where the parishioners sat in high walled pew-sections and the duty of the warden was to take down a stick from the wall and tap the head or shoulders of the snoring sleeper inside.

Until St. Paul's had its first minister, the congregation would spend Sundays listening to the schoolmaster—"a poor but virtuous Englishman by the name of John Snell"—who read prayers and sermons from books provided by Dr. Alley. If only the forthcoming minister could have the same qualities! The man unfortunately

---

10   Rev. Wade Reppert's history of St. Paul's Anglican Church was published in *The Grand Manan Historian*, No. XXI, "The Pale of the Church."

chosen by the SPG was a troublemaker who had made life difficult for everyone on Prince Edward Island before he was transferred to Grand Manan.

On taking up his new mission, Mr. Cornelius Griffin was informed that the people of Grand Manan were too poor to pay him a salary additional to that supplied by the SPG and he would be quartered in the home of Captain Ross at very reasonable terms until they could afford to build a parsonage. Mr. Griffin replied that he would purchase or build himself a house at his own expense and made lofty demands for control of the church and land, a presumption that created immediate antagonism between him and the group that had taken such pride in building St. Paul's.

Things were made worse in the spring of 1824 while he and his two sisters were travelling from Prince Edward Island to Grand Manan and he met someone who complained of church affairs under William Ross. From then on, Mr. Griffin would listen to any and all malicious gossip about the Captain, which he later passed on in a report to Saint John that was so objectionable it was not seen fit to be passed on to the SPG.

The new minister was not long in offending his congregation. After giving his formal service on the third Sunday, a large number of people from distant parts of the Island arrived to see the new missionary. Mr. Snell, the Vestry clerk, told Mr. Griffin that they had come a long way to see him and asked if he would conduct another service. He not only refused to do so but refused to even speak to them, leaving them to return home uncomforted and upset to have made the trip in vain.

In his letters to the SPG, Mr. Griffin complained of the Islanders as "being of the lowest order", "smugglers", who were "too proud to be taught their Duty to GOD and man". Matters were no better with William Ross and the members of the Vestry who were reluctant to hand over control of parish affairs and continued to work on painting the church while forming a committee to search for a makeshift parsonage. Living arrangements for Mr. Griffin and his sisters were working out badly in the Ross home where he accused Capt. Ross of being jealous of him and Mrs. Ross of condemning him for his moral preaching. As there was not room for him to keep his books inside the crowded house, he complained that they had been ruined by exposure to the elements, and the distance from his abode to the church was too far and too difficult.

In the end, the Vestry members were only able to find a small building for Griffin that was certainly unsuitable for a parsonage. For once, Mr. Griffin's complaints to the Society were justifiable.

> *Thro' the winter, we shall therefore be obliged from dire necessity to go into a most miserable fisherman's hut about 20' square—black with smoke—without any offices whatever—situate 4 miles from the Church—on rocks close by the sea shore—no fresh water near it—without a cellar (an apartment absolutely necessary in this cold climate) the tide constantly rising up under the floor and often flowing all around it, this being the place where the fishermen come ashore to gut and clean their fish in the summer season.*

There was no servant to be had on any terms, even if there had been room for one in the little building, Mr. Griffin's complaint continued.

> *I am therefore obliged with my own hands to repair the house, to fetch the water from distant brooks, or dip it up after a rain from cavities among the rocks and as no firewood can be hauled until the snow falls, we are obliged in the meantime to pick up the driftwood along the sea shore, not one of these people, when standing by and nothing to do, will condescend to assist us.*[11]

---

11 Reppert, Wade, Rev. "The Pale of the Church." *The Grand Manan Historian*, No. XXI.

This was no life for a genteel clergyman and it did not take long for Mr. Griffin to beg the SPG to remove him from the Island. The Vestry was obviously of the same mind when they met on 1 November 1824 to reaffirm to the SPG their lack of ability to provide the necessary salary or parsonage to retain his services. They prayed for more books to be sent that would allow the schoolmaster to read the liturgy and sermons after the missionary's departure.

Mr. Griffin promptly turned the request for books into a plot to fill the church with dissenting preachers and began to turn for support to the people who had spoken to him slightingly of Capt. Ross and his followers. By the end of winter, the entire church community had been divided into two bitterly opposing camps. In a turbulent meeting on Easter Monday on 4 April 1825, there was a shoving match between William Ross and Mr. Griffin, followed by shouting that ended in the meeting being adjourned. One week later, the Vestry drafted a letter to the Ecclesiastical Commissary, praying him to remove Mr. Griffin from their service, while in turn Mr. Griffin was circulating a petition demanding the Attorney General of New Brunswick bring Capt. Ross and his followers to justice for sacrilegious riot.

Moses Gerrish, now a frail old man in his 81st year, had supported Mr. Griffin in the hope that all the trouble and vexation would come to an end, but he signed the petition as one of the Justices of the Peace for Charlotte County. The Attorney General ordered more than a dozen witnesses to appear before the Court in St. Andrews where it was ruled that the charge laid by Mr. Griffin was totally groundless. The Ecclesiastical Commissary directed the missionary to remove to wherever he felt free to take accommodation away from Grand Manan. He moved to Nova Scotia in September 1825 and returned to England in 1927, where he continued to publicly revile Grand Manan and the SPG for many years to follow.

* * *

St. Paul's managed without a minister until 1832. As long as William Ross lived, the annual Vestry meetings continued as before and the religious community settled back to a more comfortable state of affairs. But on 18 August 1828 a shocking announcement was placed in the *New Brunswick Courier*:

> *Yesterday, the 13th instant, in the Grand Harbour, a short distance from their own residence, William Ross, Esquire, William Henry, James Parker and Silas Cord were upset in an open boat, which immediately sank under them. Silas Cord with much difficulty swam to shore, the other three were drowned. The bodies of Mr. Ross and William Henry have not been found.*

Death by drowning was not uncommon on this Island by the sea, as the records of the storms and shipwrecks plainly testify. It would not be long before Moses Gerrish suffered the same fate two years later, when he was 86 years old; George Russell of Seal Cove tells the story. Gerrish died of drowning when he was returning to his home by boat from Seal Cove where as Justice of the Peace he had married Joseph Plant and Elaine Robinson. Although no record of either the marriage or of Moses Gerrish's death by drowning has been found in the Grand Manan Archives, Mr. Russell vouched for its veracity by stating that Joseph Plant himself told this story to his grandfather. No grave has since been found near Gerrish's Harbour home, but there is one for William Ross erected by his wife.

William Cheney had also died earlier of apparent drowning in the passage between Harbour and Cheney Islands. But after finding his open cart and a bloodstained shirt, his family believed he had been murdered for the money he was carrying. Simeon Cheney noted: "Before Grandmother was able to tell the particulars of the death of Grand Father, the man left the Island." [12]

---

12   Cheney family papers. Grand Manan Archive, Grand Manan Museum. Grand Manan, NB.

With William Ross gone from St. Paul's, his supporters lapsed in keeping up the annual meetings and the church was left without a Vestry. Anxious to continue the Island church, Dr. Alley persuaded the Bishop of Nova Scotia, the Right Reverend John Inglis, to accompany him to Grand Manan in the summer of 1830. Impressed, the parishioners started a subscription to build a parsonage for the proposed new ministerial candidate, John Dunn of St. Andrews. In November, he made his first visit to the Island. By the spring of 1832, St. Paul's had its second and much more suitable clergyman at its helm.

Mr. Dunn was an earnest young man who was deeply conscious of his duties as a minister. Not only was he conscientious about his work at St. Paul's, but in one year after arrival he had also ministered 22 times at Seal Cove, 20 times in Castalia, and 19 times in North Head, as well as 45 times in Grand Harbour. He worked hard at keeping up and improving the parsonage for which he was partially responsible for payment despite struggling with personal debts due to the inability of the church to pay him. However, he ran into serious altercations about the use of the glebe land and this put him in conflict with some of his neighbours and his most important Vestryman, Wilford Fisher of Woodwards Cove.

Just how serious this disagreement had become was not realized until the night of 9 October 1839 when Mr. Dunn was awakened by screams from the lady living next door to the parsonage. On opening the front door, he saw, to his horror, the church was "full of flames just breaking through the eastern end ... over the pulpit window". Shortly afterwards, the fire broke through the windows and from there it went through the roof and spread over the building until the tower fell in.

As if the burning of the church was not bad enough, there was worse to come. Mr. Dunn was standing outside in the dark with Magistrate Craig who pointed to something hanging in a tree—an effigy of a man dressed in a long black waistcoat, satin vest, black pantaloons, white gloves, and black boots, with arms and legs tied to the side with cord. A note was attached to the figure lampooning Irish clergymen in Charlotte County and Mr. Dunn in particular.

In the morning after the fire, people stood around the smouldering ruins in shock. The effigy had been taken to Samuel Guptill's shop on the corner when Wilford Fisher arrived to survey the church wreckage. He walked into the shop with Vestryman Church Meigs, and was heard to remark; "I don't know anybody who wears such clothes as these on this island, but me." Pointing to the way in which the effigy had been hung by the neck, he said, "That's a hangman's knot." When Church Meigs said that in his opinion there were less than six men on Grand Manan who could tie a hangman's knot, Fisher calmly picked up a rope and showed him how it was done. Rev. Dunn reported the scene carefully in his vestry records.

In view of his arrogance at the scene of the crime and the discovery of a distinctive pipe bowl in the ruins that apparently belonged to him, Fisher and two men who worked for him were charged with

Fig. 8 – St. Paul's Anglican Church, Grand Harbour.
Built in 1840. Smokehouses in the background.

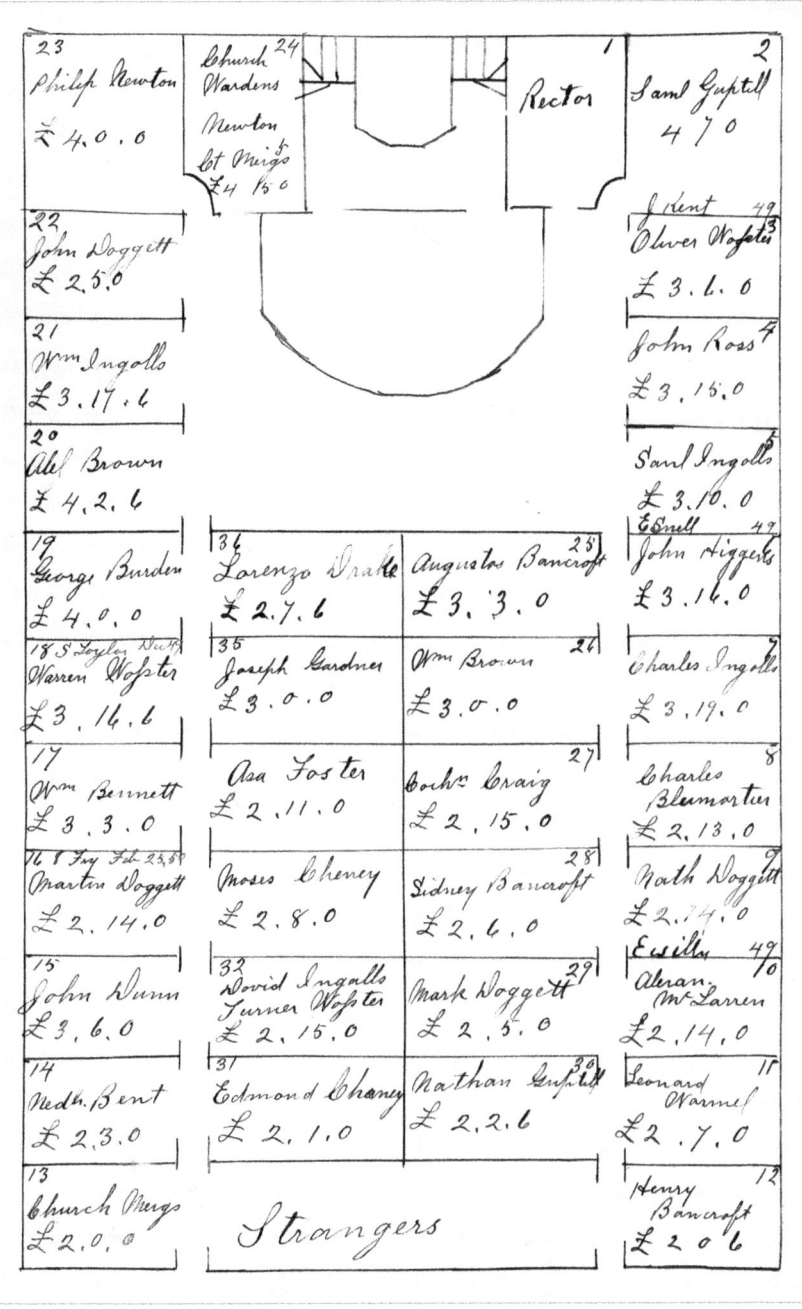

Fig. 9 – St. Paul's Anglican family pews in new church building, 1842.

the church arson. More than sixty Island men were called to St. Andrews to appear as witnesses. Public condemnation of Fisher ran high on Grand Manan, so it was a great shock when the Islanders learned that the jury "did not even leave the jury box" when it exonerated the accused.

Fisher's voice in the Vestry would sink to its lowest ebb as Mr. Dunn struggled to build a new church on the old foundation. Response to the catastrophe had been immediate and pledges to subscribe to a new building amounted to 125 names within three days, including a large sum from John Ross. Mrs. Dunn went as far as England to receive donations.

This time the church was to be made of stone. During the following winter 636 tons of rock were hauled to the site by teams of oxen. Of the 100 or so men who were involved in the construction of the new church—many from Grand Harbour—none is more memorable than Loyalist settler Oliver Wooster who, at age 72, quarried stone, made roads to haul it over, set the cornerstones of the foundation, cut staging poles and hauled them out of the woods, surveyed planking, and hauled rafting boards from Seal Cove to Grand Harbour.

By July 1840, the church was complete except for the belfry and interior decorations. The last of 400 panes of glass had been installed in the great arching windows and the Dunns would soon receive "their finest hour" on seeing the new St. Paul's ready to open its doors for the first divine service.

*   *   *

It is time, however, to close another door as we reach the end of the Gerrish/Ross saga that began it all. John Ross, the last surviving member of the founding family, had succeeded more than any of the others. As time went by, he surrounded himself with many of his sister Barbara's children in his big old house on Harbour Island. There was Elizabeth Thomas who learned to spin and make butter until she went to visit her sister Jane in 1821 and met and married Abel Ware in Athens, Maine. There was Mary Thomas who was only 22 when she had a short illness and died in her uncle's home in 1833. There was Joseph Thomas who lived there for many years with his wife and children until, for no known reason, he was killed by a man with an axe.

Joseph's daughter, Grizzy, was John's special favourite. Apparently he thought of her as a daughter and loved her dearly. She was happily married to Henry Bancroft and had two daughters of her own when she died suddenly in 1846. According to a Bancroft family story, preserved in the Grand Manan Archives, as told to Sarah E. M. Smith, sister of Allan Moses, John Ross never recovered from Grizzy's death.

> *He lost interest in everything connected with his property here. He sold Ross Island to Isaac Newton's father for a small sum that meant practically giving it away. High Duck Island, a valuable property at that time because of its weirs and numerous smokehouses, he sold out of the family entirely.*

Leaving the Island that would carry his name ever after, John Ross moved up to Saint John where he was looked after by Mary Paddock, a family cousin, no doubt the offspring of one of Capt. Thomas Ross's younger daughters. John Ross died in 1847 and was buried at Trinity Church on Thorne Avenue, Saint John.

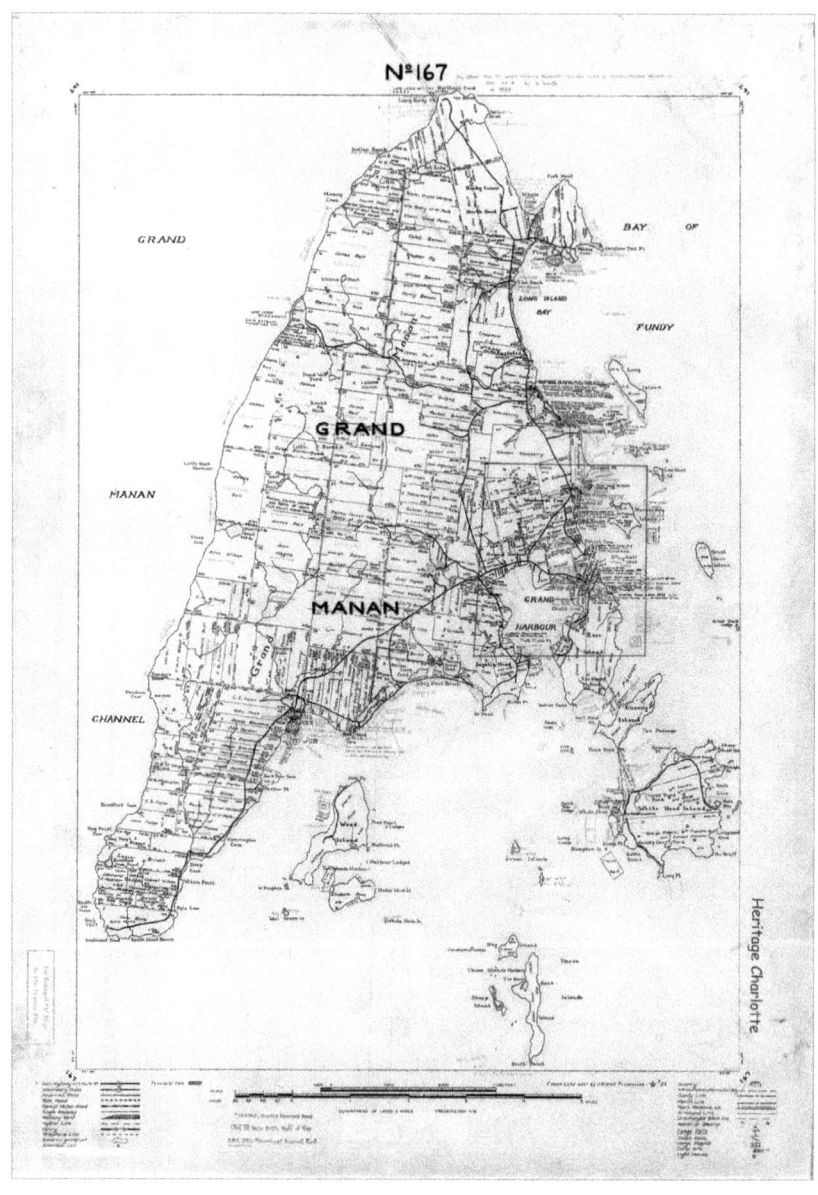

Fig. 10 – Map of Grand Manan land grants, 1833.

Chapter III
Living the Dream

Looking back from the mid-nineteenth century over the years since Moses Gerrish and Capt. Thomas Ross had arrived in Grand Harbour with their small company of United Empire Loyalists, it is time to stop and assess how successful they had been in realizing their dream. Certainly by now their successors were firmly established around the Harbour shore although their hopes for a profitable new life had to be modified to accommodate their disappointment at the infertility of the land.

None of the other Loyalist arrivals had Moses Gerrish's Harvard distinction. Most of the newcomers were of humbler origin with backgrounds in mercantile, building, logging and farming trades. But all of them had come looking for a safe haven with laws based on individual liberty and loyalty to the Crown, which they felt gave them greater hope for a better life for themselves and their children than what they feared would be the consequences of the war in America. With few exceptions, they were all Americans with strong ties to Maine. That link with their past would always remain with them even as they pushed forward into the future with their inventive understanding of the place they now called home.

Since the rocky, acidic Island soil could never be truly productive, the only way for the Loyalist newcomers to survive was to turn to the resources of the sea, beginning with modest hand-lining for pollock and cod and "torching" for herring as bait. A big change in the Harbour came with the discovery of a market for salted and smoke-cured herring sold as "bloaters". With this market came the building of two brush weirs, the "John Ross" and the "Bluebell", to catch herring off Ross Island's western shore. The prototypes for such structures had been started in Cow Passage between Cheney and White Head Islands by building wooden cribs and placing them in low tide areas before filling them with rocks and topping them with interwoven hardwood branches. With the invention of pile drivers to drive stakes into the ocean floor, brush weirs like the ones in Grand Harbour were made possible by the 1830's.

In 1850, Moses Henry Perley, Immigration Officer for Saint John, was appointed to make a *Report Upon the Fisheries of the Bay of Fundy*. When he was guided into Grand Harbour by William Frankland's pilot son, he was told that cod fishing had been good just outside Ingalls Head but had deteriorated since the advent of the weirs that had altered the flow of the herring on which the cod fed.

Grand Harbour now boasted 8 boats, each manned by 4 men, and 4 vessels crewed by 40 men in total. In his book, *Grand Manan*, Eric Allaby tells us that the boats were 17' long by 6' wide, with five birch streaks on each side of the bottom with the rest of the planks made of pine. They were small and light enough to be beached and easily hauled ashore. The hardwood bottom allowed them to be dragged over the rocks without damage. The vessels, on the other hand, could be 35' long and 10' to 11' wide, and were built to be left afloat at their moorings. They were of two types: the shallop that was only partly decked, with standing room for fishing, and the schooner that was deeper and completely decked over. Both had two sails, easy for two men to manage, and were used for cod and pollock fishing or as weir-boats.

Perley noted the large brook at the head of Grand Harbour contained great quantities of tommy cod that he was told were harvested in winter, and that the upper part of the Harbour abounded with lobsters, which could be taken with a gaff in almost any quantity during the season. The places where they could be

Fig. 11 – Herring "pinky" bound for fishing site: nets hanging over bowsprit and stern, dories on deck. Mid-1800s.

Fig. 12 – Dory fishermen hauling in lobster-pots, mid–1800s.

Fig. 13 – Fishermen hauling in herring gill-nets, mid-1800s.

found were easily identified by the holes they made digging in the clam-flats, where large clams were also abundant and could be had at low spring tides.

Up till now, there had not been much interest in fishing for lobster except for home use. In addition to being caught with gaffs, they could be taken from a small boat with spears, pitchforks, dip or hoop nets. However they were caught, they easily perished and were not suitable for faraway markets. Their main use was for fertilizer on the fields after a storm had driven piles of them up onto the beaches.

All of this changed around 1858 when John Cook, a pharmacist from Saint John, bought land from Philip Newton on the Thoroughfare Road and put up a lobster cannery that gave employment to a good number of people around the Harbour. With a ready market for his product in Scotland, he made a good profit over a few years until he decided to retire and leave everything to his son. James Cook was a kindly young man, described by Lorimer as being "too gentle to throw live lobsters into a boiling cauldron", It was not long before he closed the cannery and tried his luck at a photographic salon in Woodwards Cove. But this was not the end of lobster canning in the Harbour, as we shall see.

These were quiet years in the Harbour before and after the new Dominion of Canada was celebrated on 1 July 1867. It was during this period that the able carpenter team of Stan and Fred Carson built Isaac Newton's large Victorian mansion, which was centred along the road into Grand Harbour Village. The Loyalist desire for a good school was realized in Grand Harbour in 1865 with the construction of a handsome two-storey building. Classes were held on the lower floor, while the upper floor was used to hold meetings and dances. Long-time teacher Cochrane Craig was still employed part time during the Confederation years in addition to also carrying out the duties of Magistrate and sub-Collector of Customs.

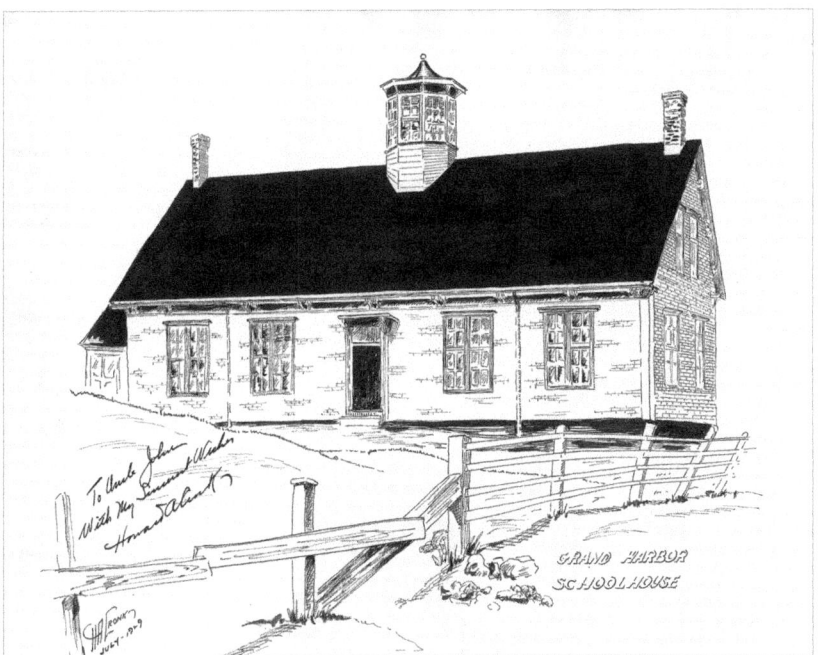

Fig. 14 – Grand Harbour Schoolhouse. Sketch by H. A. Cronk, 1929.

When Keith Ingersoll described life on "Grand Manan as part of the new Dominion" (*The Grand Manan Historian*, No. XI), he told us what each student would need for school.

> *One textbook, a slate, a slate pencil, a cloth for cleaning the slate, a water bottle for the cleaning process, a quill pen and later a steel nib with a wooden holder, and perhaps a copybook for penmanship.*

The Royal Reader textbooks had been introduced by this time. Each student advanced by reading these textbooks, which contained a wide variety of subjects ranging from poetry, literature, and history to arithmetic and elementary science. There would be many rules for the new school, including one that changed from time to time as to whether the children could or could not attend barefoot.

*   *   *

In August 1869, Spencer Baird of the Smithsonian Institute in Washington, DC, and his daughter Lucy came to Grand Harbour for the purpose of excavating the ancient shell heaps. They stayed with Simeon Cheney, grandson of first settler William Cheney, who was making a name for himself in American museums and universities for his naturalist knowledge and his abilities to be a good host. Little did the Bairds know as they packed up their Harbour findings to take back to Boston at the end of that summer that, had they planned their visit for the following summer, it would have been too late to find any sign of the middens anywhere.

As early as November 1868, Lieut. William Saxby of the British Navy had been using astronomical charts that led him to conclude that at 7 A.M. on 5 October 1869, the moon would be at that part of her orbit that was nearest the earth, making her tide attraction at maximum force. In addition, at noon of that day, the moon would be on the earth's equator, a situation that always coincided with atmospheric disturbance. Because he couldn't accurately pinpoint exactly where the tidal surges would hit, few people in Atlantic Canada heeded his warning. Thus the stage was set for the greatest storm of the century, appropriately named the Saxby Gale.

By 7:30 P.M. on the night of 4 October 1869, rain was hammering the Bay of Fundy coast driven by 100 mile an hour winds. With waves almost nine feet above the ordinary highwater level, virtually every wharf and pier in Saint John was destroyed. On Campobello Island, more than 80 buildings blew down. We have no record of the full extent of the disaster on Grand Manan Island. We know from the shipwreck reports that seven schooners were driven ashore at North Head with nine bodies floating in their wake, while parts of two small wrecked vessels were found ashore between Grand Harbour and Seal Cove with crews supposedly lost. But of the destruction in Grand Harbour, we can only imagine the devastation and desolation in the wake of the storm—how many inshore boats were damaged, how many roofs blew off barns, sheds and houses, how many buildings went down, how many people or animals were hurt! We do know, however, of the strength and resilience of the Island people. They had started with so little and done so much. We know they will build again and move on.

Isaac Newton, whose family now owned Ross Island, had been managing a store in what was left of the John Ross property. In 1870, he closed it down and had the building floated to the other side of the Harbour where it would stand on the shore beside his trading wharf in Grand Harbour Village. The village now consisted of a church, a meetinghouse, schoolhouse, customs house, magistrate's office and several stores. It lacked a blacksmith's shop, a hotel, and a cordwainer's shop[13], which were needed to meet village needs. Lorimer thought that Grand Harbour had

> *...the means within itself to form a neat, pretty village were the houses and other buildings more compact. As it is, ... being*

---

13   Shoemaker's shop

> located at nearly the central part of the island, [it] *must command a prominent position.*[14]

With the memory of the recent gale, and with the increased schooner trade at the Newton wharf and other wharves at the head of Grand Harbour, the mariners felt the need for a lighthouse to guide them safely into the Harbour and up to their individual establishments. They began to petition the government to build a lighthouse on Ross Island. In 1878, the contract for $1050 to build Grand Harbour Light was awarded to Messrs. H. H. Bowie and Co. of Saint John. Fish Fluke Point on Ross Island was purchased from Isaac Newton for $150 and Charles and George Short, master ship builders in St. Andrews, were hired to build the lighthouse. By the end of the summer of 1879, Ross Island Light, consisting of a square wooden tower 32' high with an attached keeper's dwelling, stood proudly on a rock ledge facing Ingalls Head. Veteran

---

14   Lorimer, J. G., 1876. *History of the Islands and Islets in the Bay of Fundy.* St. Stephen, NB; St. Croix Courier.

Fig. 15 – Grand Harbour Light on Ross Island, with mother and children, late 1800s.

lighthouse keeper, Henry McLaughlin, with many years of service on Gannet Rock and Head Harbour Lights, was chosen to be the Ross Island Light's first keeper. Almost ten years to the day after the Saxby Gale had torn this place apart, he lit the light on 10 October 1879.

Fig. 16 – Grand Harbour Light on Ross Island, 1965 (approx.). Photo by Gleneta Hettrick.

*   *   *

Many other buildings had been constructed in the Harbour during those ten years after the storm because the herring fishery was booming and a new design of smokehouse had transformed the industry. The new type of smokehouse was much taller than the

Fig. 17 – Smokehouse workers with smoked herring, mid-1800s.

Fig. 18 – Lobster cannery in Grand Harbour. Built in 1899 by Burnham and Morrill on the southwest side of Grand Harbour.

Fig. 19 – Ben Cossboom scooping herring in a stringing shed, mid 1900s.

previous ones and consisted of an open floor on which to build the fires and a high loft area with slatted windows in which rows of strung herring could be moved upwards from the smoke until they were perfectly done. These were the smokehouses that now mushroomed around the Harbour shore alongside the rebuilt wharves and the houses standing landward behind them.

Times were good and they would soon get better with the advent of a new lobster cannery in the centre of the village. Underwood and Company from Boston leased land from the Wooster family around the turn of the century and quickly erected a cluster of buildings to house their new business. The company employed 4 tinsmiths,

24 men and boys, and 15 women and girls, 43 people in all. By comparison, a typical Maine cannery of the time employed about 25 people. The assembly line consisted of foreman, boilers, crackers, breakers, sealers, bath-men, tail pickers, shellers, arm-pickers, fillers, crowders, weighers, coverers, and can wipers. The men manned the boilers, broke the lobsters into parts with cleavers, took the claw meat out of the shells and pushed the meat out of the tails. They were paid two to four times more than the women who picked meat from the "arm" segments with little forks and packed and weighed the cans.

When another cannery opened in Grand Harbour in 1899, we learn more about the duties of the tinsmiths from a description by Maybury Ingalls, a retired fisherman and fisheries officer from Ingalls Head who worked for the company one summer when he was thirteen years old. Burnham and Morrill of Portland, Maine, built their new cannery on the southwest side of the Harbour on property owned by Judson Guptill Sr.

As reported in "Lobsters Galore", the main building consisted of a storey and a half, with the office on the ground floor and a loft above to be used by the tinsmiths to make the cans. Maybury Ingalls's description of the tinsmith's work is quoted in "Lobsters Galore":

> *Each can had to be shaped by hand. After filling, the top was hand soldered, with each of the tinsmiths having his own charcoal fire, his soldering iron and dish of acid. It was a slow process, but the working day was from 7 in the morning until 6 in the evening, ten hours a day, 60 hours a week, so production was always good.[15]*

The rest of the cannery consisted of a shed more than eighty feet long set on piles over the water that provided areas for the coal-fired steam boilers and all the work of cooking and shelling the lobsters,

---

15   Ingersoll, L. K. "Lobsters Galore: A Brief Historical Sketch of an Important Island Fishery." The Grand Manan Historian, No. XIV.

and bathing and packing the cans. The complete staff consisted of about 30 men, women and boys, with the women and boys earning $4 a week and the men as much as $9 a week.

Only small lobsters—a minimum of nine inches from horn to tail—were used in the canning process. The shells were sold or given to farmers to spread on their land. The larger lobsters were "counters" and could be sold as "shippers" or "markets" by the fishermen. It had been discovered that fresh lobsters could be taken quickly to Eastport by boat and delivered for sale in Boston or along the East Coast of Maine to the growing number of "rusticators"—the artists and wealthy people who came out of the city in summer expecting to get fresh seafood. With the need to supply the canneries and the fresh lobster trade in Maine, the commercial fishery rose to greater and greater heights. The records of catches in 1885 were astronomical and concern began to grow that this could not be maintained after the peak had passed.

*   *   *

With the nineteenth century slowly winding to a close, we know that many things will be changing in Grand Harbour. If we look around carefully, we can see sails everywhere on this quiet water. Can we imagine that soon there will be none? For the moment, we have only to see their numbers while looking at all the working sloops and schooners assembled for the big race that began each summer in Grand Harbour, sailed out to White Head and on to Black Rock and Seal Cove Sound, through the narrows of Wood Island, and finally back into Grand Harbour for the winners to receive their awards. We can think back to Capt. Thomas Ross and his *Resolution* as we hear the names of ten captains and their vessels, with at least half of them sons of the first Loyalists as they fill the Harbour with their victorious sails.

We have had only one shipwreck disaster in Grand Harbour over the last one hundred years. It happened in the early hours of 4 July

1892 when the schooner *Cayenne* burned to the waters edge shortly after Capt. Coleman Ingalls had finished loading her with a cargo of smoked fish for New York. The uninsured remains were sold to Isaac Newton. That quiet Harbour ending should remind us that all was not always glory in the Days of Sail, especially around our rocky Island with its treacherous ledges and heavy fog. Well over 200 vessels had gone down or been valiantly rescued in the years since Gerrish and Ross first arrived, and if one added to that the number of captains and crews lost at sea it can be seen that the outer edges of our world were nothing more than watery graves.

Of the many shipwreck stories that became part of Island folklore, the most horrifying was the wreck of the *Lord Ashburton*; it was driven ashore in a snowstorm on the north end of the Island on 19 January 1857. Twenty-one men perished in that terrible disaster although eight were saved thanks to the courage of James Lawson who climbed the cliff for help and later returned to spend the rest of his days as a shoemaker in North Head.

For Grand Harbour, the most important shipwreck had to be the wreck of the *Turkish Empire*, bound for Dublin with a cargo of timber from Saint John. She ran ashore on Big Duck Island in a heavy gale on 6 March 1879 and started breaking up within five minutes. Sadly, the master and six of the crew perished, but the resurfaced vessel and cargo sold later on Grand Manan would contribute greatly to the new houses being built around the Harbour shore.

The Island shipwreck that was most cherished for its amusement was the wreck of the SS *Warwick* on Yellow Murr Ledge on the night of 30 December 1896. All the passengers and crew were saved by daylight the next day, but before the wreck disappeared from sight the frantic salvage of copious wines and spirits took on all the elements of Compton Mackenzie's 1947 novel, *Whiskey Galore*, which was based on a true story from the Outer Hebrides Islands of Scotland.

As Lloyd Cheney described it later; "Well, I was there and Gentlemen, there will never be a New Year's Day celebration [like that one]…if the world should last for a million years!"[16] Crews of small boats made chain gangs, going down in the hold of the ship and passing out cases of liquor until they were exhausted, only to find on coming back on deck that their boats were empty. One boat left for Seal Cove towing five or six bottles of various brands tied on fishing lines, with the skipper hauling in a different brand whenever he felt he needed a sip. Oh the headaches the next day!

---

16 Described by Lloyd Cheney in a letter to Keith Ingersoll of 2 February 1955 and retold in *The Grand Manan Historian*, No. XVII, "Relics of a Century: Shipwrecks at Grand Manan, Part I, 1800–1900."

Chapter IV
New Beginnings

When the clock struck midnight on 31 December 1899 in the elegant home of Isaac and Martha Newton, no one in Grand Harbour could have imagined how much the world would change in the century to come. On a nearby wall there was sure to be a gilt-framed portrait of Her Majesty Queen Victoria whose sixty-three year reign would be ending the following year as the world as she knew it slipped quietly into history.

In Grand Harbour there was already a change from Her Majesty's religion that the elite Loyalist captains had supported so faithfully over the years. Throughout the second half of the nineteenth century, a number of Wesleyan and Free Will Baptist preachers had been coming to Grand Manan and were well received on the Island. The first Grand Harbour United Baptist Church was built in 1863, followed by a larger church built in 1895 when the congregation had outgrown the smaller building, which became the parsonage.

Around the corner from the new church, St. Paul's replaced the old box pews with open-ended seating and the multi-paned windows above the altar would soon be replaced by stained glass panels. This was a busy corner in 1900 when Lawton Craig Guptill built a two-storey building to house his grocery and dry goods store on the ground floor. His family lived in an apartment on the second floor until his large home was built on the side away from the main road.

Fig. 20 – Guptill Corner, Grand Harbour, early 1900s.

Fig. 21 – Roy Ingalls house and store, Grand Harbour, early 1900s.

Fig. 22 – Holiday parade, Grand Harbour, early 1900s.

Fig. 23 – Home of Gwen Ingalls, Grand Harbour, early 1900s.

Times must have been good in Grand Harbour because 1900 also saw the opening of two more new stores in the village. Two of Isaac Newton's sons had built large homes on either side of their parent's mansion and I. L. Newton now erected another building on his property across the road from his father's mercantile business on the shore. I. L. Newton was stocked with dry goods, novelties, home furnishings, dishes, hats, shoes, and items for children. Centrally located on the Island, the store became a favourite place to visit with families, especially when Santa came in December.

Halfway between I. L and Guptill's Corner, on part of the lot first owned jointly by Oliver Wooster and John Ingalls, descendants Leroy and William Ingalls opened their general store in 1900. It stocked everything from dry goods to groceries, from work clothes to caulking for boats, plus house and farm supplies. Customers bringing their own containers could purchase kerosene and molasses.

The Ingalls brothers later added a gas pump outside their store when Edgar Sawyer and John Cronk of Grand Harbour brought the first automobile to the Island. Cars like the "Tin Lizzies" became fairly common by 1910 to 1922. Driving was not easy on the rough narrow roads, and winter snows and spring mud-sloughs closed them completely for much of the year. Horse-drawn sleighs and delivery wagons were still needed for some years to come.

Perhaps the biggest change to Grand Harbour in the Age of Locomotion was the ending of the village as a truly separate place. From now on, there would be constant traffic through this middle-of-the-Island village. Passengers and deliveries to and from Seal Cove to meet or be disembarked from the ferry in North Head made the trip there and back through Grand Harbour. When anything was needed for the Island as a whole, it was placed here for reason of its centrality, which would be both an asset and a liability for the village character.

At least Grand Harbour could rely on having good services. It had the telegraph and the telephone and before long it would have electric power when the Grand Manan Light and Power Company station was built on the outskirts of the village and proudly opened for business in time for Christmas 1929. It was joyously welcomed even if the hours were limited to late afternoon and evening, with the exception of washday Monday. Many ingenious ways were invented to connect wires for single light bulbs to hang in separate rooms or to run wires to adjoining houses to further light the darkness.

One of the prime movers for the Light and Power Company was Scott D. Guptill of Grand Harbour who was elected to the NB Legislature as a Conservative in 1912, a position he filled with honour for 23 years. Clayton Brown was the engineer in charge but we learned many years later that there had been a man from Ontario who had been present for the final work of completing the station. Sixty-five years after Christmas 1929, an elderly man came to Grand Manan and told us with a smile that when he and his sister were small their mother had told them not to be sad that their father could not be home for Christmas because "he was giving light to the children of Grand Manan".

By 1906, Grand Harbour housed the medical office and drugstore of Dr. Brougham F. Johnson and Dr. Frank D. Weldon. It was fortunate indeed that Dr. Weldon was still in the village at the end of World War I. The War to End All Wars saw close to 90 young Grand Manan men voluntarily answer Canada's call to save hapless Belgium from the invasion of 600,000 German troops in 1914. At first greeted by all with patriotic enthusiasm, the hopes for a quick war soon faded as the news came back from the boys in the cold wet trenches. Island women worked hard to knit warm socks and assemble Christmas parcels for their comfort in the terrible days of Vimy Ridge and Passchendaele.

Some of the Island soldiers were killed in action before peace was declared in 1918, and of the survivors who came home, many would be wounded for life as they struggled to continue their lives thereafter. Alas, they also brought home the 1919–1921 Spanish flu pandemic, and Dr. Weldon and Dr. Macaulay of Castalia would have their work cut out to save patients who were mostly women and children. It was said there were more fatalities from that flu than from the war, but there would have been many more on Grand Manan if those two doctors had not worked day and night to save as many patients as possible.

* * *

To turn our gaze back to the Harbour itself, the first fishing boat on Grand Manan was fitted with a gasoline engine in 1907. The reactions of the men of sail can be imagined as those first noisy, smelly contraptions made their way into the Harbour; there was much laughter and frustration when they failed to perform. It would not be long, however, before the new invention had to be recognized for its mobility and its ability to expand the range of the lobster fishery. Once installed, the weir boats kept the engine and steering aft and also used supplementary sail for some time. But with the change from sail to gasoline, the design of the lobster boats changed. The engine and tiller moved forward, leaving the rear open for standing and handling the traps. At first open-decked, it was not until 1920 that a pilothouse was built to enclose the front of the lobster boats as we know them today.

The final change in the design of the lobster boat would come after World War II due to a brilliant invention by a man who grew up in Grand Harbour, went to the little village school, attended McGill university, and eventually become Professor of Physics at Dalhousie University in Halifax. While Dr. Earnest W. Guptill was working on his PhD at McGill University in Montreal, he invented the slotted waveguide scanning unit that was used in the Lancaster bombers to spot the German U-boats during the war; it was afterwards adapted by the Canadian Marconi Company to be installed above the wheelhouse in the lobster boats as the "eyes" of the radar.

Lobster fishing no longer occurred in the Harbour after the catch yielded little or no return. By the 1920s, the fishermen were going further and further out to set their traps in season. There were new rules against catching the smaller lobsters once the canneries closed down, and more and more fresh lobsters were being shipped to Maine for the summer tourist season. The Maine lobster canners turned their attention to canning sardines, which created a good market in Eastport and Lubec for small herring that came mainly from Passamaquoddy Bay, but were sometimes also available from the many deep water weirs located outside Ingalls Head and elsewhere around the Island.

There were good years and bad years for the herring catch but the Guptill's smokehouses were kept busy in the Harbour most years. Over time, the Guptills and the Cooks would be much involved with additional smokehouses "up the Bay" in Baie Verte, Port Elgin, and Robichaud near Shediac, New Brunswick, where they caught herring in nets instead of weirs. Both families built beautiful houses in Grand Harbour to indicate their success. Smoked herring continued to have good sales in the West Indies and there was always a market for ground fish like cod, pollock, haddock and hake that were still hand-lined or caught by set trawls as in the old days

All was well on the Island until the stock market crash of October 1929. The lobster fishermen were the hardest hit as their catch was a luxury product and few were buying. There were many times when the sale of the catch would barely pay the cost of gas to go out to the traps. Grand Mananers managed to keep going throughout the Depression years with the knowledge that at least they were better off than the people in the cities. They had food on the table even if it was only "fish and tatties", and they had each other for support.

To see how much Grand Harbour Village had grown by the time of those trying years in the 1930s, we have a wonderful memory list from Howard Ingalls in which he points out who lives in every house from Ross Island to Ingalls Head and beyond. Starting out at the old Newton house and barn near Ross Island Lighthouse, he takes us across the lobster pounds to the Thoroughfare Road, still only one vehicle wide as it runs past John Cook's long ago lobster

Fig. 24 – One hundred fiftieth-anniversary memorial service at the site of the Moses Gerrish house, Ross Island, May 6, 1934.

cannery and the lane leading down to the old Philip Newton house on the point, with his barn made of timbers from the wreck of the *Turkish Empire*. Newton's wharf was made from the mast that David Romig later towed across the Harbour and donated to the Grand Manan Museum.

Howard Ingalls shows us ten residential houses on the Thoroughfare Road that include the house and big barn belonging to Hazen Dakin, who kept 15 Holstein dairy cows and a shorthorn bull much in demand for servicing cows as far away as Seal Cove and Castalia. Arthur Fleet remembered being chased by that bull and having narrowly escaped being gored by it. At sometime in the 1930s Dakin's big barn was hit by lightning and killed a horse. Ben and Allen Cossaboom helped to rebuild the barn.

Before reaching the bridge over Bradbury Brook, the last house on our right is owned by Owen and Sed Dakin, built by their father in 1902 from the money he had earned at the fish freezing operation run by the Newtons in Dark Harbour. Up to the north of the bridge on the right hand side is the Grand Manan electric power plant, with four houses on the other side including the one owned by engineer Clayton Brown. At the corner where the Lakemans live, we must pause to remember a story told to us by Otis Green about Mrs. Mint Lakeman. She and her husband Frank had earned $10,000 one year for their share in the Victoria weir. She turned to Otis Green's grandmother crying, "We're rich, we're rich, we're rich!" and reputedly threw all their old furniture in the brook in order to get new replacements!

From here we turn west to follow the road into the village centre, passing seven houses on our right, including the large Newton homes, until we reach the I. L. Newton Store. From there to Grand Brook, there are fourteen houses on the north side including Verona Ingalls/Cronk's home, the ice cream parlour, the Carriage House, owned by Capt. Irving Ingalls, the Grand Harbour School, and the Anglican parsonage.

There are no houses on the Harbour side after we cross the bridge at Bradbury Brook until we reach the new Newton Store, built in 1915. The Knights of Pythias Hall stands beside the store, after which there are thirteen houses, including the home and post office of Lyman and Martha Cheney, the home and store of Leroy Ingalls, the Herbert Daggett house/store that once held the doctor's office and pharmacy, and the combined home/store of Edwin Cheney who sold stationery and school supplies. Edwin ("Eddie") Cheney is remembered as being crippled. He had a platform with castors on which he could push himself around the store.

Staying with Howard Ingalls as he turns around Guptill's Corner heading east towards Ingalls Head, we have St. Paul's Church on our left followed by fifteen houses on the Harbour shore, with one being the site of the old lobster cannery. It is now the home of Sheldon Green, known to all as "Snooks" the diver who worked at disentangling rope in the weirs. Closer to the church, on the old William Frankland property is the home of Calvin and Elsie Brown, sales agents for a product known as Rawleigh Medicated

Ointment. They are remembered as travelling everywhere with a horse and wagon, which had a house on top for goods, and a list on the starboard side because Elsie was a very heavy woman.

There are twenty-nine houses on our right, which include the homes of bachelor Harry Cheney who served at Vimy Ridge in World War I, and Judson Foster who owns the trading vessel, *Snow Maiden*, seen often at the public wharf. Ten of the other homes belong to the prolific Green family, descendants of the first Loyalist William Green who tended sheep for William Ross on Wood Island. Oliver Ottwell Green (Ott) had grown up on Wood Island before he moved to Ingalls Head where he and his wife Nettie have a big family of twelve children, nine boys and three girls.

The Green boys would grow up to be fine fishermen. Snooks, as mentioned, was also a weir diver. Jewett became famous for his hand-carved birds and model boats, perfect down to the smallest detail. Gleason was the oldest son and was written up in Readers Digest in 1960 as the "Most Unforgettable Character I Have Ever Met" due to his many friendships within the tourist industry; in regular life he was a boat builder, devising better lines for fishing boats. Oliver "Smiles" Green, the youngest son, was written up in the November/December 2013 edition of *Saltscapes* magazine for his amazing activities at an advanced age. He had fished and worked for the provincial roads department until retirement at 65, after which he fixed engines, went clamming, worked his garden, split his own wood, and made small wooden replicas of rowboats and lobster boats and full size sleds for children. Smiles Green celebrated his 100th birthday at a surprise party at the Grand Manan Community School in December 2013; more than 600 people attended to celebrate his long and happy life.

Returning to the 1930s, we can see that Ingalls Head now consists of many Ingalls as well as Greens and on the road to our left we can find the first-built Turner Ingalls home. There is no breakwater at the end of the Ingalls Head Road at this time.

To complete the picture of the whole of Grand Harbour Village in the 1930s, we find two houses up Hill Road and five more up Foster Hill Road to the west, while going south towards Seal Cove there are fifteen houses on the right including Bob Harvey's popular blacksmith shop, a fish market, and Emerson Young's store, while on our left there are ten houses including the Crawford Guptill store on the corner beside the United Baptist Church. One is the George McLaughlin house with a barn that would be struck by lightning and burn to the ground in 1939. Further down, at the southernmost boundary of the village property, the road leads down to Long Pond Beach; it ends at Jerome Daggett's house, which will soon be sold to Sarah Briggs to create a guesthouse with outside cabins. She will sell it in the late 1960s to Mr. and Mrs. Gerald L'Aventure, who turned it into what has become Anchorage Park.

*   *   *

Leaving the village behind, we are suddenly aware that the Depression years have ended as suddenly as they began. On 1 September 1939, the Second World War began with the German invasion of Poland. Canada entered the war on 10 September, prepared to send troops to support Britain and her allies. At that time, there was only one Canadian army division for war and one for home defence. The forces were small and poorly equipped. It was not long, however, before the First Canadian Division arrived in Britain, followed soon after by the Second Canadian Division, despite the fact that their soldiers were not really needed after the fall of France.

It was agreed that Canada should put most of her manpower into the Royal Canadian Air Force (RCAF) and the Royal Canadian Navy (RCN). In 1939, there were 3,500 men in the RCN and by 1940 there were 10,000. The RCAF mounted a large training program and by October 1940 there were Canadian pilots flying Spitfires and Hurricanes in the Battle of Britain. They would become part of a special Canadian group in the RAF Bomber Command by January 1943.

By 1941, there were over 200 Grand Manan men in uniform and many more would sign up later. They readily joined all the forces. After the down years of the Depression, this was something that offered young men jobs as well as challenge and excitement. It was only later that women were also able to enlist in the war, although there was not such a great demand for nurses as there had been in World War I. Doug Daggett was among the first to sign up for the Army. He served in the Carleton York Regiment from 1941to1946, and saw action in the Battle of Italy and later in Holland and Germany. Harry Stanley of North Head joined the RCN in 1940 and was to see much action as a proud member of the original crew of the destroyer HMCS *Haida*. It ran escort duty in the North Atlantic, Bay of Biscay, and on the Murmansk run up to Russia, and was described as the "Fightingest Ship" in the Royal Canadian Navy. Reg Flagg of North Head was part of the RCAF in the RAF Bomber Command. Others, like Preston Wilcox of Seal Cove and Mac Wilson of Grand Harbour, would be doing their part, facing the threat of German U-boats, while supplying the needs of war in the Merchant Navy.

During the war years, Island fishermen going out to Georges Bank would often see German U-boats coming up around them but the fishing boats were not important enough to be troubled by them. There is one story of a U-boat surfacing and asking the fishermen for cigarettes and another of seeing the U-boat crew go ashore in a rubber boat to take fresh water from a runoff down the cliffs at the back of the Island. The only real concern at the time was for the safety of the Island ferry and the larger ships passing to and from Saint John. All lights were turned off after sunset.

We have no exact record of Island men in the ill-fated Dieppe raid in August 1942 when 5000 soldiers in the Second Canadian Division and 1000 British soldiers were landed in France. Only 2000 Canadians were rescued in the evacuation while 1000 were killed and the rest taken prisoner. With the death toll mounting, the war years continued to bring home more and more terrible news. We learn that approximately 500 men in the First Canadian Division were killed in the Allied invasion of Sicily 3 September 1943, and approximately 6000 killed in the overall invasion of Italy during the rest of the war.

Canadian soldiers fought bravely after they landed on Juno Beach in Normandy on 6 June 1944 and advanced into France ahead of the British and Americans. Their biggest battle, however, was in the fall of that year when they defeated the Germans at the Battle of the Scheldt and continued east to play a central role in the liberation of the Netherlands in 1945. The Canadian troops gave food rations to starving children and blankets to civilians during the "Hunger Winter" of 1944–45. The RCAF and RAF dropped food packages to Nazi-occupied Rotterdam, Amsterdam and The Hague up to VE Day on 5 May 1945.

Back at home, food rations for Canada had been established almost from the beginning of the war in order to send supplies to Britain. Sugar was soon made scarce and there was a strange stipulation that bakery bread should not be sliced. The Grand Manan Cookbook has many recipes like "War Cake" that go back to that time of having to make do with less. It would take time after the war ended to get back to normal and certainly the Island stores expected a sugar rush when rationing and price controls ended.

Recovery for everything on the Island came with the end of World War II when the boys came home and the tourist trade picked up and people were buying lobsters again. From all accounts, the post war years were halcyon times for Grand Harbour Village. From 1947 to 1949, the main road was paved all the way down the Island from North Head to Seal Cove and people danced in the street at the opening ceremony in the village. They danced regularly in the new Knights of Pythias Hall, built across the road from the Anglican Church, and they saw movies and plays when the hall was turned into a cinema with ten rows of seats. They spent many happy times eating "the best hamburgers in the world" in Ruth Wooster's "The Barn" café further up the road—a fine meeting place for boys from the other villages to meet Grand Harbour girls and vice versa. Lobster fishing and sales were good and Grant Dakin's smokehouse business was doing exceptionally well on the Thoroughfare Road.

Grand Harbour had two schools in 1948 when the new Grand Manan High School was built. The land donated by Lyman Cheney for the school was part of the original huge Cheney/Doggett Lot

Fig. 25 – Grand Manan High School, Grand Harbour. Built in 1967.

that had formed half of the main village area. The school was open for classes that September but not officially complete until the official opening ceremony in May 1949. The old school further down the road was kept as the Elementary School until 1967 when a new and larger High School had to be built, turning the first High School into the Elementary School. The old Grand Harbour School was demolished. Many people were sad to see the end of their old school. Gleason Green told us he had attended classes without shoes. Smiles Green remembered how they all slid down the hill towards the Harbour in winter to walk the two miles home along the old road near the shore.

The Canadian Legion bought the old I. L. Newton store and housed the Allan Moses bird collection for the summer before the Grand Manan Museum was built to house it in the Centennial Year of 1967. The Moses family were latecomers to Grand Manan, arriving in North Head in 1872. They came from England with a background in taxidermy and natural history, which led to the establishment of a small family museum near their home. They bought Simeon Cheney's Nantucket Island and continued his interest in entertaining scientific visitors. Allan Moses grew up with a love of ornithology, which gave him the opportunity in 1923 to join the Labrador Patrol, recently established to curb sea bird poaching along the north shore of the St. Lawrence River estuary, a spectacular place in which to see thousands of gannets, kittiwakes, guillemots, puffins, and murres nesting on high cliffs and remote islands. This was the area Audubon explored in 1833 after visiting William Frankland on White Head Island.

Following his summer Labrador patrol, Allan Moses took up employment to collect specimens in Labrador and the Cape Verde Islands for the Cleveland Museum of Natural History, which in turn qualified him to join a Rockefeller Foundation expedition to Tanganyika in 1928 to search for the rare African green broadbill that the American Museum of Natural History wanted for its bird collection. Allan Moses was lucky enough to be the one who collected it on 26 July 1929. As a reward, Sterling Rockefeller promised him support for establishing Kent Island, Grand Manan, as a protected nesting site for endangered eider ducks. He cared for the eiders until Bowdoin College took over Kent Island in 1935. Moses continued to collect specimens for American museums and the Moses Museum in North Head until he was nearly seventy, when he began to be concerned about the future of his exhibits.

The Moses Memorial Museum of Natural History opened 17 October 1951 in the basement of the Grand Manan High School; shortly afterwards, the National Film Board came to Grand Manan to film Allan Moses in *The Birdman of Grand Manan*. Sadly, he died on 23 March 1953, three weeks before the world premiere of this delightful short film was shown to a packed local audience in Knights Theatre in Grand Harbour. When grade twelve was added to the High School in the 1960s, attendance increased and there was no longer room for the Moses Memorial Museum. The new and larger High School was built in the Centennial Year of 1967, and the Grand Manan Museum, proudly housing the important Allan Moses bird gallery, opened its doors to the public for the first time.

Fig. 26 – Grand Manan Museum temporary location in former I. L. Newton store, Grand Harbour, mid 1960s.

The new Museum included much in the way of post-Loyalist displays in its main gallery, featuring kitchen furniture and utensils, spinning wheels, and other much loved memorabilia.

Fig. 27 – Grand Manan Museum, Grand Harbour. Built in 1967.

It added a typewriter in tribute to American author, Willa Cather, who built a summer cottage in the 1920s on part of the land once owned by Barbara Ross Thomas near Whale Cove in North Head. The Walter B. McLaughlin Marine Gallery was added in 1979 to exhibit the fishing industry and shipwreck displays as well as to show off the magnificent crystal lens from Gannet Rock Lighthouse.

Before the Museum was enlarged again in the 1990s, we have another story to tell relating to the past. One day in July 1992, an imposing man stepped inside the doors of the Museum and announced he was the direct descendant of Joel Bonney and his son, Alexander, who was the first white child born on Grand Manan. He was Thomas Britain Hamilton of Kitchener, Ontario. He told us he played the bagpipes, so nothing would do but to have him stand outside, as tall and good looking as his patriarchal ancestor, piping his celebratory music for all to hear.

* * *

Everything seemed normal on the Island on an early morning at the beginning of February 1976. It was simply business as usual until the wind picked up around midday. After that, all hell broke loose. Like the Saxby Gale of 1869, the Groundhog Day Gale of 1976 came in from the south, bringing high tides with it, but this time there was no warning. Gusts were soon recorded as blowing as hard as 146 miles per hour. Waves crashing into Ingalls Head wharf exploded 150 feet into the air and two cars belonging to brothers Murray and Maurice Guptill were blown off into the sea.

All around Grand Harbour, wharves and fish processing stands were collapsing. One smokehouse that had doors open on the windward side exploded as if a bomb had gone off. The tides rose seven feet above the predicted high water level and many boats were badly damaged. A boat that had been hauled up onto a field for the winter was carried across the Harbour and grounded out on

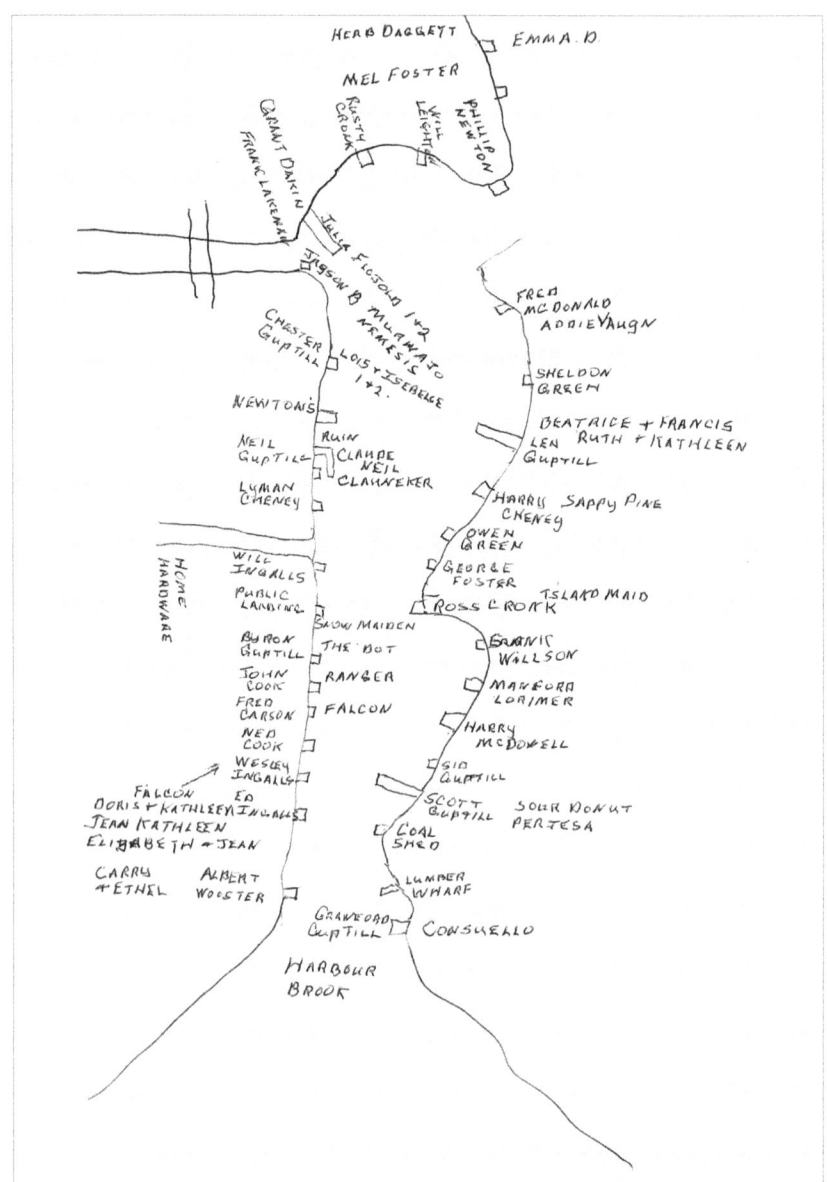

*Fig. 28 – Grand Harbour wharf sites before Groundhog Day Gale 1976.
Drawn from memory by Junior (Owen) Ingalls.*

the Little League baseball diamond located by the Newton Store.
Sheds and lobster traps were smashed to pieces and the old brush
weirs off Ross Island disappeared under the waves.

FISH PLANT, GRAND MANAN

Fig. 29 – Dakin fish plant, Grand Harbour, 1970

By the time the tide had receded, the wreckage of all the buildings, fish stands, gear sheds, and boats, which had been funnelled by the wind and tide across Grand Harbour from one side to the other, ended up stranded on the Thoroughfare Road in the northwest corner. The whole Grant Dakin enterprise and shore was gone under the shapeless mass of flotsam. So heavy was the tangled timber debris that the government grader had to be brought in to clear a path to allow the traffic to get through.

Miraculously, with all the damage done in the Harbour and elsewhere on the Island, not a single injury was reported. But with millions of dollars lost by the fishing industry, it seemed that Grand Manan would never be the same again. Certainly, looking around the Harbour that day from the perspective of those long ago Ross Island settlers, it would seem as if it had all been for nothing. So much had gone in just one day. So much that had been built up and succeeded and prospered over the years was now a heap of smashed up remains.

But if the children and grandchildren and great grandchildren of the Loyalist ancestors had learned anything over time, it had been how to survive despite their difficulties with the merciless wind and sea. They had coped with their disappointments over the lean and rocky land and they had faced the challenging distances to and from faraway trading ports. They had survived the Saxby Gale and they would do the same with the Groundhog Gale. They would have to make another new start, building on the old foundation as they had with the Anglican Church after the fire, and make the rebuilding bigger and better.

As we near the two hundred year mark since the Loyalists arrival, we can see that there is much to be thankful for in Grand Harbour Village after the storm has passed. There are the Grand Manan Elementary and High Schools, a new Wesleyan Church on the site of the old elementary school, the Anglican and United Baptist Churches, a first class Museum, a Legion Hall, a bank, a fire station, a police station, a funeral parlour, as well as an extension of the Ingalls Store to include hardware and building supplies for all the new Island houses. Verona's ice cream parlour is now the popular Harbour Gifts Store and the Newton Store is still doing well. There are two garages for servicing motor vehicles.

At Grand Harbour's southernmost boundary, Anchorage Park is flourishing as a tourist campground under the management of the Province of New Brunswick. Ingalls Head is now an official part of the village and the burgeoning wharf will be crowded with handsome lobster boats on the second Tuesday in November when the fleet departs at dawn to set their traps for another successful season.

Moses Gerrish can rest in peace as we go across to Ross Island on 6 May 1984 to join four hundred Islanders in a memorial service to honour his name and those brave souls who came with him or followed his lead. Their United Empire Loyalist hopes for a good life on Grand Manan Island have succeeded beyond their highest dreams.

Notes and Acknowledgements

Grand Harbour is no longer a separate village since it became amalgamated into the Island-wide Village of Grand Manan in 1995. But I have a special affection for this modest, middle-of-the-Island place. It seems to me to be the cornerstone of Island life and stands for stability. It has been my home for over thirty years and I have always been grateful for the privilege and joy of living here.

I wish to say a fervent thank you to all the people who have made this book come to be. I am most grateful to Carole Guptill, Jeanne Ingalls, Ray Ingalls, and Bud and Marian Fleet for their help with interviews. I am especially grateful to all the people who answered my many questions as well. Special memorial thanks go to Otis Green who drove around the Harbour with me on several occasions and taught me so much about life in the village as he knew it for so many years. Personal thanks go to Jocelyn Taylor and Liz Edgar for their kindness while I was ill at the start of the writing, to Ludger Müller Wille for his eternal support and encouragement as it proceeded, and to Bill Edgar who made it all possible with his rescue missions around my ancient computer.

I would like to thank Joan Harvey for giving us so much Grand Manan news and information in her monthly editions of the *Island Times*. My appreciation extends as well to the writers of Island related articles for the *Telegraph Journal* in Saint John and for the *News and Chronicle* in St. Stephen, all of which I found helpful in writing this book.

Thanks for the kind assistance of Archivist, Ava Sturgeon. I have drawn on a great deal of genealogical material in the Grand Manan

Archives, housed in the Grand Manan Museum. These records contain much in the way of maps, letters, newspaper articles, family trees, and items of general interest information. These archival records are carefully and continually brought up to date by a team of volunteers who deserve a lot of praise for their patience and diligence.

Much of the background to the main story has been taken from the splendid series of historical information publications produced by the Grand Manan Historical Society. Listed below are the issues of the *Grand Manan Historian* that were most used as references:

IV. Grand Manan: A Summer Reminiscence (1868) by B.F. DeCosta.

V. The History and Settlement of Grand Manan by Jonas Howe.

VIII. Report of a Royal Commission on the State of Grand Manan Fisheries (1836)

IX. The Robb Report on the state of the fisheries, the condition of the lighthouses, the contraband trade, and various other matters in the Bay of Fundy (1840)

X. Perley Report on the fisheries of Grand Manan (1850)

XI. Grand Manan as part of the New Dominion (1867)

XIII. At the Turn of the Century (1877–1905)

XIV. Lobsters Galore. A Brief Historical Sketch of an Important Island Fishery by L. K. Ingersoll.

XV. The Rich and the Lean Years (1906–1939)

XIX. Memorial Issue (p.18–26. A General Report on Applications for Land by Donald McDonald, 1 January 1806)

XXI. Pale of the Church, by Wade L. Reppert.

XXV. MD for the Islands: The Life and Times of Dr. John Francis Macaulay (1876–1939), by L.K. Ingersoll

XXVI. Shipwrecks of Grand Manan, by Eric Allaby, M.L.A

Issues IV and V were under the editorship of Buchanan Charles. Issues VIII to XIX were edited and contained introductions and notes by Keith Ingersoll.

Bibliography

For further reading, I found the following publications interesting and useful:

Allaby, Eric, 1984, 1995, *Grand Manan*. Grand Manan, NB; Grand Manan Museum.

American Friends Service Committee, 1989. *The Wabanakis of Maine and the Maritimes: A Resource Book about Penobscot, Passamaquoddy, Maliseet, Micmac and Abenaki Indians*. Bath, ME; American Friends Service Committee, New England Regional Office.

Baird, S. F., 1882. *Notes on Certain Aboriginal Shell Mounds on the Coast of New Brunswick and of New England*. Washington, DC; Smithsonian Institution.

Condon, Ann Gorman, 1984. *The Loyalist Dream for New Brunswick*. Fredericton, NB; New Ireland Press.

Cronon, William, 1983. *Changes in the Land: Indians, Colonists and the Ecology of New England*. New York; Hill and Wang.

Dixon, Chester A. 1958 (Nov.). "Island Courier Section". St. Stephen, NB; *St. Croix Courier*.

Grand Manan Museum, 2019. *The Story of the Bicentennial Quilt, 1784–2019*. Grand Manan, NB; Grand Manan Museum.

Hogg, Elaine Ingalls, 2007. *Historic Grand Manan*. Halifax, NS; Nimbus Publishing.

Ingersoll, L. K., 1963. *On This Rock*. Grand Manan, NB; Gerrish House Society.

Ingersoll, L. K., 1991. *Wings Over the Sea: The Story of Allan Moses*. Fredericton, NB; Goose Lane Editions.

Leefe, John, 1978. *The Atlantic Privateers*. Halifax, NS; Petheric Press.

Lorimer, J. G., 1876. *History of the Islands and Islets in the Bay of Fundy*. St. Stephen, NB; *St. Croix Courier*.

Mowat, Grace Helen, 1953. *The Diverting History of a Loyalist Town*. Fredericton, NB; Brunswick Press.

Rhodes, R., 2004. *John James Audubon: The Making of an American*. New York; Vintage Books.

Rivinus, E. F. & Youssef, E. M., 1992. *Spencer Baird of the Smithsonian*. Washington, DC; Smithsonian Institution.

Russell, George H., 1930. "Old Stuff", (Series of Island history articles). St. Stephen, NB; *News and Chronicle*.

Illustrations

Figures 1 & 2 – Maps by Ragnar Müller Wille

Figures 3–9, 11–27, & 29 Courtesy of Grand Manan Archives

Figure 10 – Map of land grants, 1833. Courtesy of Heritage Charlotte. www.heritagecharlotte.com

Figure 28 – Courtesy of *Island Times*, April 27, 2020

Author photo by Anneke Gichuru (pg 89)

Cover photograph by Peter Cunningham (pg 93)

About the Author

Wendy Dathan has lived on Grand Manan Island for over thirty years but began life long ago and far away in a bauxite mining camp in the forested interior of Guyana. With the end of World War Two, her parents placed her in a boarding school in England. Six years later, she was reunited with her family in Montreal where she received her BA in English and Geography from McGill University in 1955.

Married in Scotland in 1957, she and her husband returned to Montreal to bring up their two sons in Pointe Claire. She took up the study of botany, specializing in edible wild plants, which led to teaching and working in the Plant Science Department at McDonald College as well as employment at the McGill University Herbarium.

In 1984, she returned to McGill for an MA in Geography and spent the following summer researching The Canadian Reindeer Project in the Northwest Territories and Alaska. As a result, she later wrote *The Reindeer Botanist: Alf Erling Porsild, 1901–1977*, a major biographical study of one of Canada's most important Arctic research scientists and eventual Curator of Botany at the National Museum of Canada. *The Reindeer Botanist* was published by the University of Calgary Press in 2012 and won the Clio Prize for Northern Canadian History in 2013. She is also the author of three additional books: *Bauxite, Sugar, and Mud: Memories of Living in Colonial Guyana, 1928–1944; Swallowtail Calling: A Naturalist Dreams of Grand Manan Island; My Dust Will Dance: The Adventurous Life of Joanne Pauline Barberis.*

Wendy has travelled widely over North America on natural history field trips. She discovered Grand Manan in 1978 on a trip to study puffins and returned as often as she could until making it her permanent home in 1988. She became Curator of the Grand Manan Museum during its expansion years and immersed herself happily in learning about Island life and history. As one Grand Mananer put it, "She didn't know much when she came but she has learned some since then!"

After retirement in 2000, she opened a small art shop and continued biographical writing. *A Harbour for the King* is her tribute to the place she feels privileged to be at home and where she lives quietly in her old house by the sea.

About Eric Allaby

Eric Allaby is an underwater archaeologist, marine artist, and former Curator of the Grand Manan Museum. He served as a member of the New Brunswick Legislative Assembly from 1987 to 2006. His forthcoming book, *The Sea Wins: Shipwrecks of the Bay of Fundy*, will be published in the fall of 2022. His marine art can be seen at www.facebook.com/ericallabymarineart

About the Cover

The cover photograph of the Grand Harbour shoreline with slight fog lifting is by Peter Cunningham.

He has been visiting and photographing Grand Manan since childhood. (See CBC story at: www.cbc.ca/news/canada/new-brunswick/nb-grand-manan-photos-1.4114784)

More information on Peter Cunningham's photography can be found at his website. www.petercunninghamphotography.com. He lives in New York City but calls Grand Manan "my primary heart place".

Cover photograph, uncropped

www.ingramcontent.com/pod-product-compliance
Lightning Source LLC
Chambersburg PA
CBHW051541120626
46551CB00013B/1327